THE GOOD ENERGY MANAGER'S GUIDE

74 checklists for practical energy management

TREVOR BOUTALL

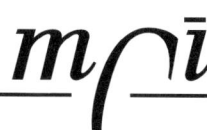

Request for Comment

We would like to know what you think of this guide and how you are using it. We are particularly interested to know of any way in which its content, language, style or layout could be improved so that it would better meet your needs.

Please send your comments to: MCI, Russell Square House, 10-12 Russell Square, London WC1B 5BZ.

Acknowledgements

Thanks to Louise Evans, Bryan Fowler, Penny Foxton, Colin Haycock, Karen Marshall, Joe McCullagh, Beryl Nelms, John Pooley, Mike Roberts for contributing to the text and production of this guide.

Thanks also to the thousands of managers who tested drafts of the checklists.

Copyright

© 1994, 1995 Trevor Boutall, except the text of the Management Standards themselves which are Crown Copyright © 1989 - 95 inclusive.

All rights reserved. No part of this publication may be reproduced, stored in a retrieval system, or transmitted in any form or by any means, electronic, mechanical, photocopying, recording or otherwise, without the express permission of the Copyright owner.

Neither the author nor publisher make any representation, express or implied, with regard to the accuracy of the information contained in this book and cannot accept any legal responsibility for any errors or omissions that may be made.

Published by the Management Charter Initiative, the operating arm of the National Forum for Management Education and Development, Russell Square House, 10-12 Russell Square, London WC1B 5BZ. Registered Charity No. 1002554.

Special Distributor: The Institute of Energy.

The Good Energy Manager's Guide
ISBN 1 897587 24 4

Contents

How to use this guide	5

Energy Management	7
What is Energy Management?	8
Advising on Energy Strategy	11
Appraising Energy Management	13
Identifying and Evaluating Opportunities for Improvements	17
Providing Advice on Energy Strategies	21
Measuring Energy Performance	25
Championing Energy Efficiency	29
Promoting the Efficient Use of Energy	31
Encouraging Commitment to Energy Efficiency	35
Supporting Energy Efficiency	39
Providing Energy Efficiency Advice	41
Providing Advice on Measuring Energy Performance	45
Supporting Continuous Improvement in Energy Usage	49
Purchasing Energy	53
Selecting Suppliers	55
Contracting for Supply	61

Operational Management	67
What is Operational Management?	68
Managing the Operation	71
Meeting Customer Needs	73
Managing Change	79
Quality Assurance	85
Time Management	87

Managing People   89
   Personnel Planning   91
   Developing Teams and Individuals   97
   Managing Teams and Individuals   105
   Working Relationships   111
   Managing Problems with Staff   117
   Equal Opportunities   121

Managing Finance   125
   Managing Budgets   127
   Cost Control   131

Managing Information   133
   Using Information   135
   Meetings   141

National Standards   145
   What are National Standards?   146
   Standards for Managing Energy   148
   Middle Management Standards   150
   Links between the Checklists and the Standards   152

Keywords Index   155
Useful addresses   160

How to use this guide

Energy management is about ensuring the most efficient use of energy resources in your organisation. Whether you are a full-time energy manager or a general manager who has special responsibility for energy management, you will find this book describes what you have to do. Knowing what you have to do is the essential first step to being effective.

As an energy manager, you are often required to perform a number of functions simultaneously for which you need a wide repertoire of skills and a broad suite of technical knowledge as well as common sense. You are required to respond to new developments and fast-changing circumstances, and to work at many different levels.

The Good Energy Manager's Guide breaks down the energy manager's role into simple, practical checklists to help you tackle energy management tasks successfully. There is no magic in it, just crystal clear objectives and strictly logical steps.

The checklists can be used for a variety of purposes, such as job descriptions, recruitment, appraisal schemes and performance management. However, they are designed, first and foremost, to help you do your job. Here are some examples of how you might use them.

Addressing unfamiliar tasks

You may be faced with a task you have not performed for a long time, or perhaps never met before. Take selecting a new energy supplier, for example. How would you go about it?

The contents page tells you that, under *Purchasing Energy*, there is a section on *Selecting Suppliers*. There are 5 checklists to help you. *Selecting potential suppliers* helps you identify possible suppliers in

Contents
- ▶ Purchasing Energy
  - ▶ Selecting Suppliers
    - ▶ 5 checklists

line with organisational and legal requirements. *Obtaining bids* and *Obtaining tenders* describe the tendering process. *Clarifying and improving offers* helps you identify the best offer and *Deciding on supplier* helps you arrive at a fair and satisfactory decision.

Tackling important tasks

You may have to do something critically important which you want to ensure you get right - running an important meeting for instance.

Keywords Index
▶ Meetings
▶ Leading
▶ Leading meetings

The keywords index at the back of the book points to the checklist for *Leading meetings*. This helps ensure you get the best from all participants, arrive at well-informed decisions and get there in the fastest possible time.

Checking that you are doing things properly

Assessing your organisation's energy efficiency performance may be something you do on a regular basis but you may like to check occasionally that you are doing things properly.

Contents
▶ Advising on Energy Strategy
▶ Measuring Energy Performance
▶ Assessing energy efficiency performance

The contents page shows there is a section on *Measuring Energy Performance* under *Advising on Energy Strategy*, with a checklist specifically for *Assessing energy efficiency performance*. There are also useful checklists to help you develop monitoring systems and collect and record information.

Carrying out a public task

Some aspects of energy management are more public than others, so it is important not just to get it right, but to be seen to get it right.

Keywords Index
▶ Achievements
▶ Publicising
▶ Publicising energy efficiency achievements

For example, *Publicising energy efficiency achievements* involves presenting your organisations achievements to the world at large, and needs careful preparation to ensure your information is accurate, relevant to the audience and positions your organisation in the best light.

You should find checklists to cover all your energy management tasks. They are based on the national Standards for Managing Energy developed by the Management Charter Initiative (MCI). If you can prove you are competent in the areas covered by the checklists, you could qualify for units towards a national vocational qualification. Refer to pages 146-149.

Energy Management

What is Energy Management?

The key purpose of energy management is to ensure the effective management of energy resources to meet the organisation's objectives.

As an energy manager you have to support senior management and operational managers in your organisation by providing information, advice and guidance to help them develop strategies, operational plans and working practices which make the most efficient use of energy. You also have a missionary role, promoting the benefits of energy efficiency and developing a supportive culture. You may have the responsibility for purchasing energy supplies and managing relationships with your suppliers as well.

Many managers have to balance the responsibility for energy management with an operational or line management role. The checklists on Operational Management on pages 67-143 of this book will help you in this role.

Energy management involves providing information to senior managers to help them develop business plans and strategies which use energy in the most efficient way. To do this you have to assess your organisation's current performance and measure this against best practice and the potential for improvement. You need to advise senior management how to devise strategies and how best to implement them. You must then agree targets for energy usage and put in place the systems accurately to measure your organisation's energy performance.

A key part of any energy strategy is gaining people's commitment to using energy efficiently. You will need to be clear about the tangible benefits of energy efficiency to the organisation and present these benefits to managers and the workforce. By helping people identify and develop the skills they need, you will gain their commitment to using energy most efficiently.

Much of an energy manager's time is spent providing on-going advice to people about how they can use energy efficiently. Advice given at the planning stage can help ensure that energy efficient working practices are adopted. However, people also need advice and support in measuring energy usage, and in taking corrective action where usage exceeds that planned. As an energy manager you need to stay abreast of developments, innovations and best practice in the wider environment and assess how these can lead to continuous improvements in energy usage in your organisation.

If you have responsibility for purchasing energy, you will need to ensure that you follow organisational and legal requirements in securing reliable and cost-effective energy supplies. You will need to develop, and often negotiate, relationships between suppliers, users and technical experts, especially when there are problems or failures in supply.

Energy Management

Advising on Energy Strategy	Championing Energy Efficiency
Appraising Energy Management Identifying and Evaluating Opportunities for Improvements Providing Advice on Energy Strategies Measuring Energy Performance	Promoting the Efficient Use of Energy Encouraging Commitment to Energy Efficiency

Supporting on Energy Efficiency	Purchasing Energy
Providing Energy Efficiency Advice Providing Advice on Measuring Energy Performance Supporting Continuous Improvement in Energy Usage	Selecting Suppliers Contracting for Supply

Energy management is a demanding role, requiring technical knowledge of a wide range of principles, methods and data. It also requires well developed skills in handling the variety of people and situations you have to deal with. No two energy managers' jobs are exactly the same. Very often the role is not clearly defined and the responsibility for energy management has to be juggled with a range of other operational priorities. This book will help you define your role and provide some simple, practical guidelines for tackling the situations in which you find yourself as an energy manager.

Advising on Energy Strategy

Advising on Energy Strategy is about providing senior management with complete and relevant information to help them determine your organisation's strategies, policies and plans for the efficient use of energy. It involves:

Appraising Energy Management   **13**

    Assessing current energy management performance   14
    Assessing the scope for improvement   15

Identifying and Evaluating Opportunities for Improvements   **17**

    Identifying opportunities to improve energy efficiency   18
    Evaluating and advising on opportunities to improve
        energy efficiency   19

Providing Advice on Energy Strategies   **21**

    Providing advice on formulating strategies   22
    Providing advice on implementing strategies   23

Measuring Energy Performance   **25**

    Developing monitoring systems and processes   26
    Collecting and recording information   27
    Assessing energy efficiency performance   28

Energy Management

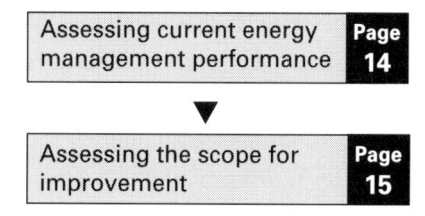

Appraising Energy Management

This section is about knowing how your organisation is doing in terms of energy management and what its potential for improvement is.

The checklists will help you to:

- assess your organisation's current level of commitment to, and effectiveness in, energy management
- identify the scope for improvements in energy management and energy usage in your organisation.

The process for *Appraising Energy Management* looks like this:

| Assessing current energy management performance | Page 14 |

▼

| Assessing the scope for improvement | Page 15 |

Appraising Energy Management

Assessing current energy management performance

1. **Identify your organisation's level of commitment to energy management** - what is your organisation's current commitment to energy efficiency and what are its energy strategies?

2. **Assess the people in your organisation** - have individuals and teams got the ability to achieve relevant energy efficiency targets?

3. **Examine and evaluate your organisation's current activities and operations** - in respect of energy usage, management and performance.

4. **Identify your organisation's energy efficiency initiatives** - what are your organisation's current initiatives and what are the processes for developing them? Discuss with the people directly involved.

5. **Identify the statutory requirements** - what are the statutory requirements which affect the use of energy throughout your organisation's activities? Statutory requirements may include Health and Safety at Work Act, COSHH, Environmental Protection Act, integrated pollution control, Fuel/Electricity Control Act, Clean Air Act.

6. **Evaluate your organisation's energy efficiency initiatives** - how do these fit with your organisation's strategies and with the relevant statutory requirements?

7. **Identify roles and responsibilities in developing performance indicators** - discuss and agree these with the people concerned.

8. **Agree performance indicators** - agree clear, relevant and assessable performance indicators for energy usage, costs and efficiency. Present these in formats which meet organisational requirements.

Appraising Energy Management

Assessing the scope for improvement

1. **Evaluate the results of energy audits** - if you have undertaken energy audits, what do the results show about how you could make more efficient use of energy in your organisation?

2. **Evaluate current and prospective operational activities** - what are their implications for energy usage, efficiency, safety? What effects might they have on resources, the environment, waste, work practices and procedures?

3. **Identify and evaluate current energy sources** - are they the most appropriate and effective sources of energy for the activity for which they are being used?

4. **Evaluate the effectiveness of your monitoring procedures** - are your monitoring and auditing processes capable of revealing areas for improvement?

5. **Assess potential areas and scope for energy savings** - discuss these with the people involved.

6. **Prioritise your findings** - evaluate the areas where improvements will have the greatest impact, consistent with your organisation's objectives.

7. **Present proposals for improving the effectiveness of energy usage** - present proposals in a form which helps people to take informed decisions.

Identifying and Evaluating Opportunities for Improvements

This section is about spotting opportunities for improving energy efficiency and assessing ways of implementing them.

The checklists will help you to:
- identify opportunities to make more efficient use of energy in your organisation
- evaluate whether and how to implement these potential improvements in your organisation
- advise others on possible improvements to the efficient use of energy.

The process of *Identifying and Evaluating Opportunities for Improvements* looks like this:

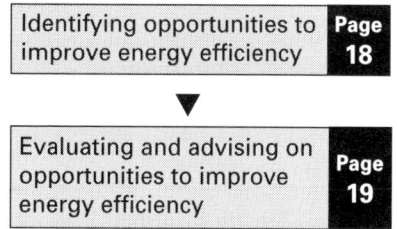

Identifying and Evaluating Opportunities for Improvements

Identifying opportunities to improve energy efficiency

1. **Regularly review current resources, systems and activities in your organisation** - look for opportunities to improve energy efficiency.

2. **Identify developments and advances in best practice in the wider environment** - see if any new products, services, technological innovations or innovative working practices could help improve energy efficiency in your organisation.

3. **Choose the most energy efficient resources** - select and use resources (such as finance, people, premises, equipment, materials and energy supplies) which make best use of energy.

4. **Identify opportunities for recycling or recovering energy** - what are the implications for operational activities?

5. **Identify initiatives which support energy efficiency programmes** - there may be grants, environmental measures, local, national or European initiatives which can support your organisation's programme.

6. **Encourage people to identify opportunities** - which improve energy efficiency and contribute to the effective use of energy and a sustainable environment.

7. **Participate in developments** - actively seek ways of involving yourself and your organisation in developments and innovations in energy efficiency.

Identifying and Evaluating Opportunities for Improvements

Evaluating and advising on opportunities to improve energy efficiency

1. **Evaluate opportunities to improve energy efficiency** - weigh up the advantages and disadvantages (such as safety, cost, reliability, environment, quality) in relation to your organisation's systems and practices.

2. **Assess advances in technology** - how applicable are they to your organisation's operations and activities?

3. **Evaluate purchasing opportunities** - make sure you maximise advantages in selecting energy resources.

4. **Monitor your organisation's systems** - and evaluate how effective they are.

5. **Provide advice and make recommendations** - based on your evaluations and in line with your organisation's requirements.

6. **Seek further advice** - if you are unable to make clear recommendations, ask appropriate people for further information and advice.

Advising on Energy Strategy

Providing Advice on Energy Strategies

This section is about providing advice to senior management on developing and implementing organisational strategies for the efficient use of energy.

The checklists will help you to:
- provide relevant and accurate advice to help senior management formulate energy management strategies
- provide information and advice to help senior management decide on the best way of implementing energy management strategies.

The process of *Providing Advice on Energy Strategies* looks like this

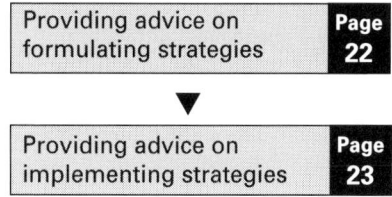

Providing Advice on Energy Strategies

Providing advice on formulating strategies

1. **Offer advice based on relevant, accurate and up-to-date information** - relevant information may include energy cost statements, management information systems, monitoring and targeting records, best practice guidance, codes of practice, legislation.

2. **Consult appropriate internal and external sources of information** - especially where you need additional information.

3. **Take account of your organisation's aims, objectives and activities** - make sure you take account of all relevant factors such as strategic aims, operational objectives and activities, design issues and maintenance requirements when giving your advice.

4. **Outline realistic targets for savings and improvements in energy usage** - identify and explain the implications of these targets for organisational activities, aims and objectives.

5. **Define the responsibilities for energy management** - discuss and agree to whom energy management responsibilities are devolved.

6. **Describe a culture of energy efficiency** - provide advice on developing the right culture within your organisation.

7. **Clearly state the benefits to the organisation** - your advice will be more readily accepted if the benefits of energy efficiency are clearly understood.

8. **Document your advice** - keep a record of your advice in line with organisational requirements.

Providing Advice on Energy Strategies

Providing advice on implementing strategies

1. **Identify options for implementing energy strategies** - discuss the options (such as publicity, training, motivation and instruction) with decision makers.

2. **Weigh up the options** - what are their various advantages and disadvantages in terms of safety, cost, reliability, environment and quality?

3. **Select methods of implementation** - make sure these are consistent with your organisation's strategies for energy efficiency in accordance with management's requirements.

4. **Identify the resources required to implement strategies** - what resources (such as finance, people, equipment, energy supply, premises and materials) will you need to implement the strategies in your organisation?

5. **Present the options and your recommendations** - in a manner which helps people take informed decisions.

Advising on Energy Strategy

Measuring Energy Performance

This section is about evaluating how efficient your organisation is in its use of energy and measuring its progress towards its energy efficiency targets.

The checklists will help you to:
- develop appropriate and reliable systems and processes for measuring your organisation's energy efficiency performance
- collect valid and sufficient information
- analyse that information and assess your organisation's energy efficiency performance
- make realistic recommendations for improving that performance.

The process of *Measuring Energy Performance* looks like this:

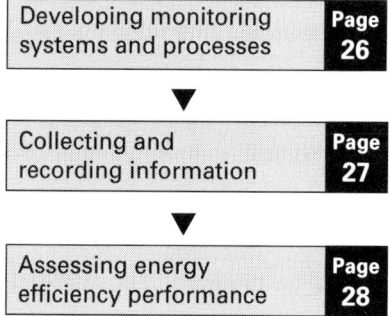

Measuring Energy Performance

Developing monitoring systems and processes

1. **Be clear about the objectives** - discuss the reasons for developing monitoring systems and agree the scope of the evaluation of energy usage with the relevant people.

2. **Include all critical aspects** - make sure monitoring systems and processes cover all key factors which affect the evaluation of energy usage.

3. **Identify appropriate measures, tools and techniques** - choose performance measures and assessment tools and techniques which allow you to evaluate energy usage accurately.

4. **Identify sources of information on energy used** - are these valid, reliable and sufficient to make an accurate evaluation?

5. **Review existing internal sources of information** - check whether existing sources are satisfactory before establishing new systems.

6. **Identify resources required to develop new systems** - gain approval and check out availability of the resources needed to implement new systems.

7. **Produce clear and accurate documentation** - covering the whole of the monitoring systems and processes.

8. **Provide adequate and accurate information** - make sure all relevant people are informed about the evaluation.

Measuring Energy Performance

Collecting and recording information

1. **Obtain sufficient information** - make sure you have sufficient, relevant information on a regular basis in order to allow you to make an accurate and complete analysis.

2. **Investigate any weaknesses, confusions or discrepancies in the information** - and take appropriate action to get information of the quality you require.

3. **Take into account information from suppliers** - in your analysis, use any information you can get from suppliers on the energy efficiency of your products, services and processes.

4. **Encourage people to provide information** - encourage teams and individuals to provide information which contributes to the evaluation and improvement of energy performance.

5. **Record information carefully** - store complete and accurate information according to organisational requirements.

Measuring Energy Performance

Assessing energy efficiency performance

1. **Use accurate, relevant and timely information** - on your organisation's energy efficiency performance.

2. **Use appropriate methods of assessment** - which allow you to interpret and evaluate information about performance accurately.

3. **Base your analyses and forecasts on relevant information** - make all your criteria and assumptions clear in your report.

4. **Report on your organisation's performance on a regular basis** - and make sure these reports are received by the appropriate people and provide sufficient information for them to take decisions.

5. **Identify areas for improvement** - and compare your organisation's current performance with current best practice.

6. **Make recommendations for improvement** - make realistic recommendations in line with your organisation's energy management strategies and policies and communicate these to senior management.

Championing Energy Efficiency

Championing Energy Efficiency is about gaining people's commitment by communicating the benefits of, and the role people can play in, achieving the efficient use of energy. It involves:

Promoting the Efficient Use of Energy — 31

    Promoting energy efficiency in your organisation — 32
    Publicising energy efficiency achievements — 33

Encouraging Commitment to Energy Efficiency — 35

    Supporting and encouraging people to use energy more efficiently — 36
    Providing advice on the skills required for the efficient use of energy — 37
    Providing advice on training and development — 38

Promoting the Efficient Use of Energy

This section is about promoting the efficient use of energy both inside and outside the organisation.

The checklists will help you to:
- gain people's commitment to energy efficiency by identifying the benefits of energy efficiency to your organisation and the individuals who work in it
- publicise the benefits of energy efficiency and your achievements both inside and outside your organisation.

The process of *Promoting the Efficient Use of Energy* looks like this:

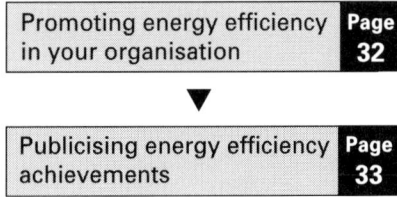

Promoting the Efficient Use of Energy

Promoting energy efficiency in your organisation

1. **Identify and evaluate the features associated with the efficient use of energy** - look at factors such as costs, quality, productivity, the environment and safety, and assess their relevance to your organisation's objectives, values and culture.

2. **Identify opportunities to promote the efficient use of energy in your organisation** - select and exploit those opportunities most likely to maximise energy efficiency throughout your organisation.

3. **Communicate the benefits of the efficient use of energy effectively** - think about the people you are communicating with and present the benefits in the way that will be most appealing to them.

4. **Publicise energy efficiency achievements** - and promote these throughout the organisation.

5. **Clarify roles and functions** - make it clear what each part of the organisation can do to help use energy most efficiently.

6. **Gain individual commitment** - help individuals to understand how they can support your organisation's drive for energy efficiency.

7. **Identify champions** - get senior managers to communicate their support for developing a culture of energy efficiency and conservation to the workforce.

Promoting the Efficient Use of Energy
Publicising energy efficiency achievements

1. **Look for opportunities to build external awareness** - evaluate opportunities to create and sustain awareness of energy efficiency outside your organisation. Do these opportunities contribute to your organisation's objectives? Are they consistent with its values and culture?

2. **Publicise your organisation's achievements** - make sure your information is current and consistent with your organisation's strategy and policy.

3. **Think about your audience** - communicate your organisation's achievements in a way which is relevant and useful to your audience.

4. **Promote the business benefits** - show how energy efficiency leads to the continued improvement and effectiveness of your organisation.

5. **Encourage feedback** - get people to tell you what they think and respond appropriately.

Encouraging Commitment to Energy Efficiency

This section is about getting people involved and making sure they have the necessary skills to use energy efficiently.

The checklists will help you to:

- gain people's commitment to, and involvement in, the efficient use of energy
- identify the standards of performance and the skills required to achieve your organisation's energy efficiency plans
- assess the needs of teams and individuals for training and development
- provide advice on training and development

The process for *Encouraging Commitment to Energy Efficiency* looks like this:

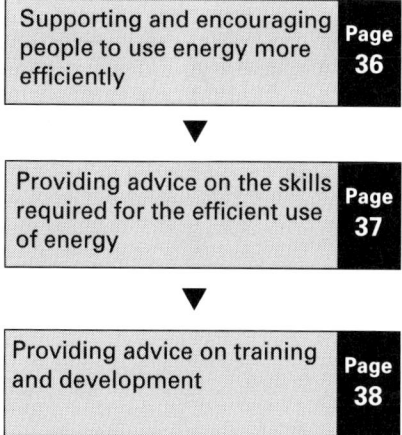

Encouraging Commitment to Energy Efficiency

Supporting and encouraging people to use energy more efficiently

1. **Provide useful information on energy efficiency initiatives** - make sure all documentation is clear, relevant, sufficient and accessible.

2. **Help people understand their role** - encourage individuals and teams to contribute to the definition of their own role and responsibility with regard to the efficient use of energy.

3. **Get people involved** - invite people to offer their suggestions, ideas and views and get them to take an active part in improving energy management in your organisation.

4. **Give reasons when a recommendation is not accepted** - where it is not possible to act on people's recommendations, provide clear and relevant reasons as soon as possible.

5. **Publicise examples of good practice** - in energy efficiency within your organisation.

6. **Lead by example** - make sure your own behaviour at work demonstrates your commitment to the efficient use of energy.

Encouraging Commitment to Energy Efficiency

Providing advice on the skills required for the efficient use of energy

1. **Provide information on the skills and standards of performance required** - make sure you give accurate and up-to-date information on what is required to achieve your organisation's energy management plans.

2. **Seek relevant views** - encourage individuals and teams to contribute and offer suggestions.

3. **Provide accurate advice** - make sure your advice is consistent with your organisation's overall strategy and plans for energy usage.

4. **Present your advice clearly** - think about the people to whom you are giving advice and communicate in a way which promotes understanding and acceptance.

5. **Take into account resource limitations** - your advice will not be credible if it ignores resource constraints.

6. **Take into account equal opportunities** - make sure your advice provides equality of opportunity and does not discriminate unfairly.

7. **Provide the opportunity for questions** - allow people to seek clarification or voice any areas of concern.

Encouraging Commitment to Energy Efficiency

Providing advice on training and development

1. **Encourage people to evaluate and meet their own needs** - provide help for teams and individuals to evaluate their own needs in the effective use of energy and to find ways of meeting those needs.

2. **Identify training requirements** - working with the teams and individuals concerned, assess their training requirements against the standards of performance required.

3. **Establish relationships** - with providers of training and development.

4. **Provide appropriate advice** - give advice to teams and individuals to plan activities to meet training and development needs.

5. **Encourage feedback** - encourage people to give you feedback on training and development activities and to make recommendations on how these can be improved.

6. **Make improvements where necessary** - where training and development activities prove to be unsuitable or ineffective, make improvements for the future.

Supporting Energy Efficiency

Supporting Energy Efficiency is about making sure everyone in your organisation has the right information, advice and support to be able to use energy in the most efficient way. It involves:

Providing Energy Efficiency Advice	**41**
Providing advice on developing energy efficient plans	42
Providing advice on energy efficient practices	43
Providing Advice on Measuring Energy Performance	**45**
Supporting the development of performance measurement systems	46
Supporting the collection, analysis and documentation of information	47
Supporting Continuous Improvement in Energy Usage	**49**
Evaluating information relating to continuous improvement in energy usage	50
Providing advice on developments and improvements in energy usage	51

Providing Energy Efficiency Advice

This section is about giving people advice on the efficient use of energy at work.

The checklists will help you advise people to:
- consider the implications for energy efficiency in their planning
- consider the impact their working practices have on the efficient use of energy
- adopt more efficient working practices.

The process of *Providing Energy Efficiency Advice* looks like this:

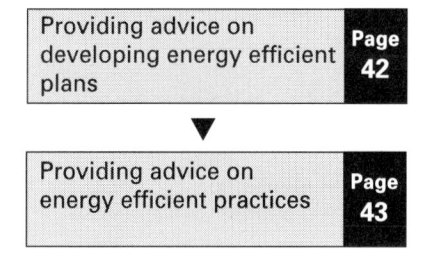

Providing advice on developing energy efficient plans	Page 42

▼

Providing advice on energy efficient practices	Page 43

Providing Energy Efficiency Advice

Providing advice on developing energy efficient plans

1. **Offer a planning advice service** - encourage people to ask for your advice on the efficient use of energy when they are developing their operational plans.

2. **Provide relevant and timely advice** - based on up-to-date and accurate information.

3. **Take into account resource limitations** - your advice will lack credibility if it does not recognise resource constraints.

4. **Monitor the energy performance of plans** - monitor whether the targeted energy performance is achieved in the implementation of the plans.

5. **Advise on any corrective action required** - discuss the resulting energy performance with the relevant people and advise them to amend plans, where necessary.

Providing Energy Efficiency Advice

Providing advice on energy efficient practices

1. **Provide accurate and up-to-date information** - give individuals and teams the latest information on the actual and potential impact of working practices on energy performance.

2. **Encourage people to evaluate and improve working practices** - get individuals and teams to evaluate the effects of their own working practices on energy performance and take action to improve these practices, if appropriate.

3. **Develop suitable monitoring systems** - develop systems which measure the impact of working practices on energy performance.

4. **Monitor changes in working practices** - evaluate the effects and whether changes in working practices really lead to improved energy performance.

Providing Advice on Measuring Energy Performance

This section is about helping people to develop systems for measuring energy performance and to collect and analyse information about energy usage.

The checklists will help you to:
- help people develop appropriate performance measurement systems
- help people collect relevant information and interpret it.

The process of *Providing Advice on Measuring Energy Performance* looks like this:

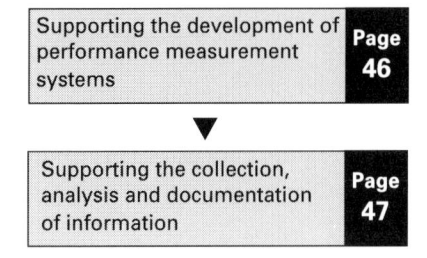

| Supporting the development of performance measurement systems | Page 46 |

▼

| Supporting the collection, analysis and documentation of information | Page 47 |

Providing Advice on Measuring Energy Performance

Supporting the development of performance measurement systems

1. **Identify your organisation's performance indicators for energy usage** - in partnership with the people involved.

2. **Identify your organisation's current methods for measuring energy performance** - in partnership with those involved.

3. **Encourage people to evaluate their targets** - provide information and advice which encourages people to evaluate the validity and effectiveness of your organisation's current energy performance targets.

4. **Present information and advice in an appropriate way** - think about the person to whom you are giving information or advice and communicate in a way which promotes understanding and acceptance.

5. **Encourage people to develop clear and concise criteria** - help people to produce clear and concise criteria for measuring energy performance.

6. **Encourage people to collect regular and timely information** - get people to collect information on the effectiveness of the systems on a regular and timely basis and to make recommendations for improvements.

Providing Advice on Measuring Energy Performance

Supporting the collection, analysis and documentation of information

1. **Identify the support required** - identify and agree with individuals and teams the nature and extent of the support they require.

2. **Provide clear advice** - give clear advice on appropriate energy management tools and techniques, and how to collect and record data.

3. **Help with analysis and interpretation** - provide relevant advice on the analysis and interpretation of data.

4. **Ensure availability of necessary documentation** - provide support to ensure that necessary documentation is available within agreed timescales.

5. **Provide appropriate support** - think about the people you are helping and provide support in a way which is acceptable to them.

6. **Encourage feedback** - encourage and assist people to give you feedback on the collection, analysis and interpretation of information and to ask you for help when they need it.

Supporting Continuous Improvement in Energy Usage

This section is about helping people in your organisation become ever more efficient in their use of energy.

The checklists will help you to:
- support people in meeting their energy performance targets
- advise people on developments and improvements they could make in their energy usage.

The process for *Supporting Continuous Improvement in Energy Usage* looks like this:

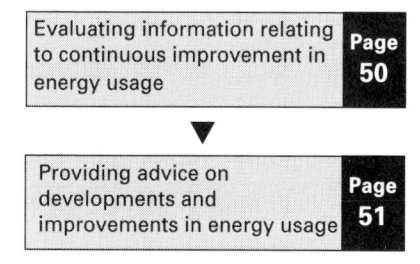

Evaluating information relating to continuous improvement in energy usage	Page 50

▼

Providing advice on developments and improvements in energy usage	Page 51

Supporting Continuous Improvement in Energy Usage

Evaluating information relating to continuous improvement in energy usage

1. **Check the validity of monitoring and analytical techniques** - make sure your techniques for monitoring and analysing energy usage allow you to spot opportunities for improvements.

2. **Provide accurate information** - give sufficient information to allow conclusions to be drawn.

3. **Obtain additional information** - where information is insufficient, get additional information to improve the evaluation.

4. **Take corrective action as soon as possible** - act quickly where problems are identified in achieving energy efficiency targets.

5. **Offer advice to those not meeting energy performance requirements** - make sure your advice is relevant, timely and contributes to improvement.

6. **Refer unresolved problems to the appropriate people** - advise people clearly and accurately of any unresolved issues and record the details in accordance with organisational procedures.

Supporting Continuous Improvement in Energy Usage

Providing advice on developments and improvements in energy usage

1. **Assess the results of monitoring, evaluations and audits** - what are their implications for your organisation's activities?

2. **Give results to relevant people** - communicate these results and their implications to decision makers clearly and accurately.

3. **Identify trends and developments in the use of energy** - and communicate these to the relevant people.

4. **Advise people of the potential impact on their activities** - let people know the possible impact of trends and developments in energy usage on their activities.

5. **Identify the potential benefits of improvements** - discuss the potential benefits, balanced by any resource implications, with the relevant people.

6. **Encourage decision makers to adopt suggestions for improvements** - the support of senior managers will motivate individuals in your organisation to be involved in the effective management of energy.

7. **Inspire and empower people** - communicate information in a manner and form which promotes enthusiasm for the management of energy and allows them to take informed decisions.

Purchasing Energy

Purchasing Energy is about securing reliable and sufficient supplies of energy, services, equipment and plant on the most favourable terms possible. It involves:

Selecting Suppliers   55

    Selecting potential suppliers   56
    Obtaining bids   57
    Obtaining tenders   58
    Clarifying and improving offers   59
    Deciding on supplier   60

Contracting for Supply   61

    Negotiating supply agreement   62
    Establishing a contract for supply   63
    Placing a contract for supply   64
    Dealing with contractual claims   65
    Resolving problems in supply   66

Purchasing Energy

Selecting Suppliers

This section is about selecting suppliers for the supply of energy, services, equipment or plant. The same process can be used to select suppliers for any commodity, product or service.

The checklists will help you:
- draw up a list of potential suppliers
- obtain bids or tenders which can be evaluated accurately and fairly
- clarify any points in offers which are unclear
- improve on these offers where possible
- select the most appropriate supplier.

The process of *Selecting Suppliers* looks like this:

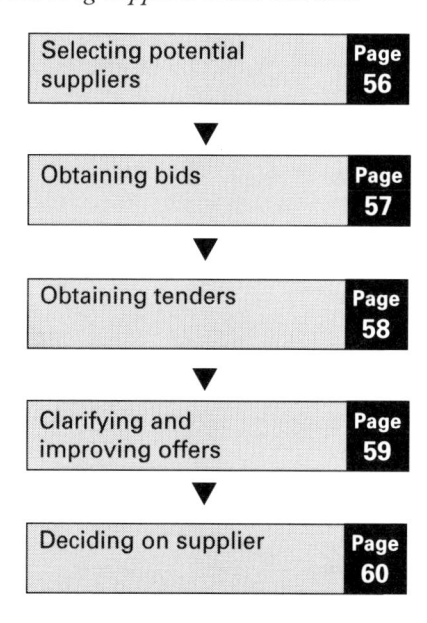

Selecting potential suppliers	Page 56
▼	
Obtaining bids	Page 57
▼	
Obtaining tenders	Page 58
▼	
Clarifying and improving offers	Page 59
▼	
Deciding on supplier	Page 60

Selecting Suppliers

Selecting potential suppliers

1. **Identify potential suppliers** - make sure you draw up your list of potential suppliers in line with organisational policy and legal requirements.

2. **Develop selection criteria for those invited to quote** - in line with organisational policy and legal requirements.

3. **Invite potential suppliers to quote** - make sure the number and range of suppliers is in line with organisational policy and legal requirements appropriate for specified supplies.

4. **Establish selection criteria for the successful supplier** - in line with organisational policy and legal requirements.

Selecting Suppliers

Obtaining bids

1. **Draw up a clear specification** - check that it conforms to relevant legal requirements.
2. **Invite potential suppliers to bid against the specification.**
3. **Ask for bids in a standard format** - this will allow for easy comparison of bids.
4. **Be clear about the procedures and timetable for submitting bids** - check that these procedures are followed.
5. **Resolve queries** - from potential suppliers promptly.

Selecting Suppliers

Obtaining tenders

1. **Draw up tender documents** - in line with organisational policy and legal requirements.
2. **State the specification of supplies and conditions of contract** - state specifications clearly and accurately.
3. **Give full information on procedures for submission of tenders.**
4. **Advertise the tender** - in line with organisational policy and legal requirements.
5. **Obtain sufficient tenders** - make sure that adequate competition has been secured.
6. **Receive, record and open tenders** - following organisational procedures and legal requirements.
7. **Resolve queries from tenderers promptly and fairly.**

Selecting Suppliers

Clarifying and improving offers

1. **Promptly resolve any queries over variances from specification** - in line with organisational policy and contract terms and conditions.

2. **Obtain advice on any variances from specification** - ask users and technical staff about the implications of any variances.

3. **Raise any queries relating to conditions of supply promptly** - clarify the situation with the supplier and record it accurately.

4. **Consult between users, suppliers and purchasers** - in line with organisational policy and professional requirements.

5. **Determine the scope and content of any negotiation** - this may well be constrained by the method of obtaining the offer.

6. **Negotiate improvements to conditions of supply and confirm these with the supplier** - conditions of supply may include price, quantity, quality standards, carriage and delivery, maintenance and after-sales service, method of payment and terms of payment.

Selecting Suppliers

Deciding on supplier

1. **Evaluate offers against established criteria** - in line with organisational policy and legal requirements.
2. **Fully document - your decision and reasons for this decision.**
3. **Communicate your decision promptly** - to users, suppliers and other interested parties.
4. **Use performance rating accurately in the selection of suppliers** - if you are using a system of rating the performance of suppliers, use this accurately and fairly.

Contracting for Supply

This section is about finalising a contract for the supply of energy, services, equipment or plant. The same process can be used to finalise a contract for the supply of any commodity, product or service.

The checklists will help you to:
- negotiate a valid contract with conditions which are advantageous to your organisation
- establish clear, agreed and legally-binding terms within the contract
- place the contract with your chosen supplier
  deal with any claims arising from the contract.

The process for *Contracting for Supply* looks like this:

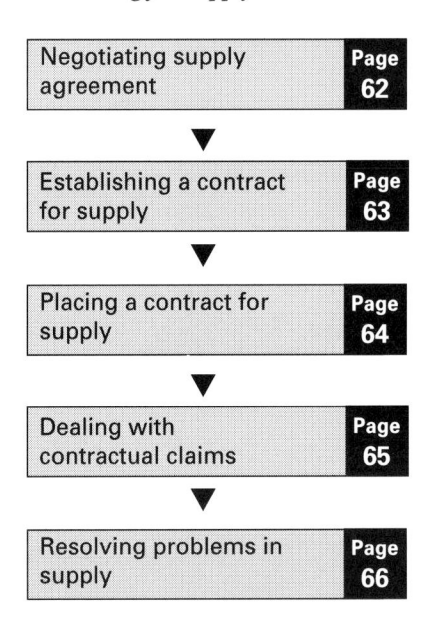

Negotiating supply agreement	Page 62
Establishing a contract for supply	Page 63
Placing a contract for supply	Page 64
Dealing with contractual claims	Page 65
Resolving problems in supply	Page 66

Contracting for Supply

Negotiating supply agreement

1. **Ensure that the supply agreement meets established criteria.**
2. **Ensure that the supply agreement conforms with organisational policy and legal requirements.**
3. **Ensure that the negotiation results in savings to your organisation.**
4. **Conduct negotiations in a professional manner.**
5. **Evaluate the results of negotiations against your objectives** - and learn from your experience.
6. **Agree arrangements for the management of supply agreements** - with both suppliers and users.

Contracting for Supply

Establishing a contract for supply

1. **Ensure the contract is valid and legally binding**
2. **Seek appropriate legal advice where necessary** - and act upon it.
3. **Ensure the contract offers adequate protection and acceptable risk regarding any possible breach of contract.**
4. **Clearly establish criteria for determining failure to supply -** and state the agreed remedies within the contract.

Contracting for Supply

Placing a contract for supply

1. **Complete the contract accurately** - include all necessary information.

2. **Send the completed contract to the supplier** - adhere to agreed targets, budgets and timescales.

3. **Obtain approval for the contract from the person with designated authority.**

4. **Resolve any queries on the contract promptly** - and provide feedback to user and supplier.

5. **Send the contract via the means agreed.**

6. **Obtain appropriate acknowledgement of receipt** - of the contract and approval of its content.

7. **Distribute copies of the contract** - to users and other designated staff.

Contracting for Supply
Dealing with contractual claims

1. **Investigate any claims** - establish whether they are valid or not.
2. **Clarify any queries on claims promptly with contracting parties.**
3. **Seek appropriate legal advice** - and act upon it when necessary.
4. **Document claims accurately.**
5. **Communicate the reasons for the claim** - tell relevant parties promptly the circumstances which gave rise to the claim.
6. **Refer claims to the designated person** - if the claim is outside your authority.

Contracting for Supply

Resolving problems in supply

1. **Tell suppliers promptly about any complaints by users.**
2. **Identify the cause of the problem.**
3. **Discuss the problem quickly** - try to resolve the problem promptly by discussing it with suppliers and users.
4. **Tell someone in authority about the problem.**
5. **Seek legal advice on the problem if necessary.**
6. **Obtain alternative supplies** - if the problem results in failure to supply.
7. **Take action to redress the unsatisfactory supply** - take appropriate action according to the terms of the contract.
8. **Negotiate any alterations to terms and method of payment with suppliers and users** - and record these accurately.
9. **Take action to ensure that future supplies will meet user specification.**
10. **Record problems and how they were resolved** - tell users about them and include these in your appraisal of your supplier's performance.

Operational Management

What is Operational Management?

The key purpose of management is to achieve the organisation's objectives and continuously improve its performance.

Operational management is being clear about the objectives you have to achieve through your team, in your department or for your part of the business; and using the available resources to best effect.

It involves managing the operation of your part of the organisation as effectively as possible; being clear about what you are expected to deliver; designing systems and procedures; and organising the workplace to achieve this. Always you need to be looking for, and implementing, ways of doing things better to provide a quality service or product every time.

Operational management means getting things done through people. You have to make sure you have the right people to do the job. You have to develop a team and help each member of the team develop the skills they need to perform their job effectively. You need to plan the work and allocate it amongst the team, setting individual objectives and providing feedback on their performance. Managing people involves building effective working relationships and dealing with difficult problems, being careful to be fair and equitable in all your dealings.

As a manager, you will often be required to prepare budgets for the expenditure, and perhaps income, for your part of the operation. It is your responsibility to ensure that these financial targets are met and that all staff are aware of how they can help in improving the financial performance. Operational management also involves obtaining and using information to aid decision-making; and leading and participating effectively in meetings to arrive at decisions.

Operational Management

Managing the Operation
Meeting Customer Needs
Managing Change
Quality Assurance
Time Management

Managing People
Personnel Planning
Developing Teams and Individuals
Managing Teams and Individuals
Working Relationships
Managing Problems with Staff
Equal Opportunities

Managing Finance
Managing Budgets
Cost Control

Managing Information
Using Information
Meetings

Operational management is a complex business requiring a range of skills and knowledge, together with disciplined time-management, if you are to succeed. However, the checklists in this book provide some simple, practical guidelines for effectively tackling everyday tasks. You will find them relevant whether you are a team leader, supervisor or manager at any level, although you may find your role is to contribute to, rather than have full responsibility for, an activity.

Operational Management

Managing the Operation

Managing the Operation is about working out ways of meeting customer requirements on time, every time. It involves:

Meeting Customer Needs   73

    Establishing and agreeing customer requirements   74
    Maintaining supplies   75
    Maintaining a productive work environment   76
    Meeting customer specifications   77
    Solving problems for customers   78

Managing Change   79

    Identifying opportunities for improvements   80
    Assessing the pros and cons of change   81
    Negotiating and agreeing the introduction of change   82
    Implementing and evaluating changes   83

Quality Assurance   85

    Assuring quality   86

Time Management   87

    Managing your time   88

Operational Management

Meeting Customer Needs

This section is about maintaining an effective operation to meet customer needs.

The checklists will help you to:
- be clear about the needs of your customers
- ensure suppliers provide value for money
- maintain a safe and efficient working environment
- design your operational systems to meet customer specifications
- solve problems for customers when things go wrong.

The process of *Meeting Customer Needs* looks like this:

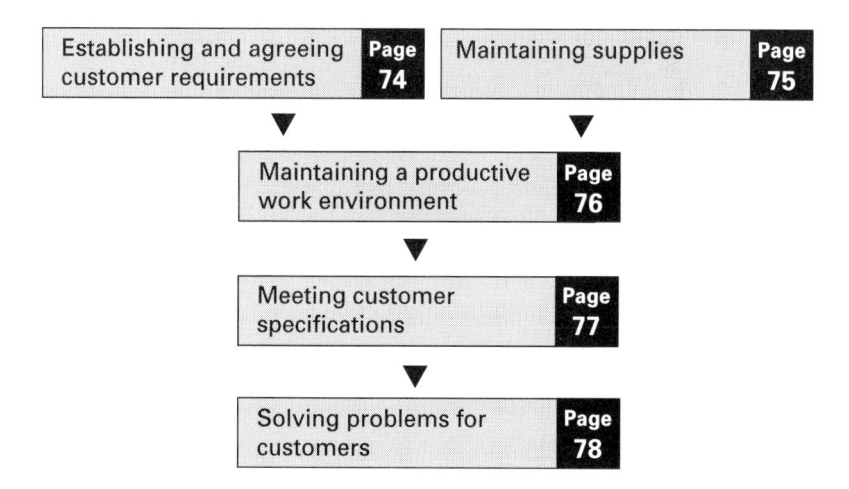

Establishing and agreeing customer requirements	Page 74

Maintaining supplies	Page 75

Maintaining a productive work environment	Page 76

Meeting customer specifications	Page 77

Solving problems for customers	Page 78

*Refer to the section on **Purchasing Energy** (pages 53-66) for more checklists on **Selecting Suppliers** and **Contracting for Supply**.*

Meeting Customer Needs

Establishing and agreeing customer requirements

1. **Research your customers' needs** - use formal and informal techniques to identify the services or products your customers, or potential customers, need.

2. **Design your services or products to meet your customers' needs** - and ensure your services and products meet legal and organisational requirements and resource constraints.

3. **Describe your services or products clearly** - explain your services or products to customers, think about the person you are talking to, and make sure you communicate in a manner and at a pace which is appropriate.

4. **Encourage customers to discuss their requirements** - invite them to seek clarification wherever appropriate and tell you how well you are meeting their needs.

5. **Communicate frequently with customers** - develop a relationship of trust and goodwill, and keep them informed about any changes which affect them.

6. **Ensure agreements meet legal and organisational requirements** - consult specialists if you are in doubt.

7. **Negotiate effectively** - use your experience of past negotiations to ensure the success of future negotiations.

8. **Optimise agreements** - create a 'win-win' situation, where you achieve your objectives whilst meeting customer needs.

9. **Draw up detailed specifications** - ensure that specifications of customised services or products contain all the relevant information to allow customer requirements to be met.

10. **Keep accurate records** - include all relevant information about customer agreements and implementation plans.

11. **Design customer-focused operations** - organise your operations to provide the most efficient service to your customers.

12. **Develop helpful staff** - encourage your staff to put the customers first and to take personal responsibility for meeting customer needs.

Meeting Customer Needs

Maintaining supplies

1. **Identify the supplies you need** - check they are sufficient to meet customer requirements.

2. **Identify and develop suitable sources of supply** - make sure your suppliers can provide you with the materials you need for your product and services; always have alternative suppliers available for contingencies, if possible.

3. **Select suppliers objectively** - apply fair criteria in choosing your suppliers.

4. **Review your suppliers regularly** - check they continue to offer best value for money and quality of service.

5. **Keep accurate records of suppliers and supplies** - keep a complete list of suppliers' details and monitor levels of supplies regularly.

6. **Watch market and economic trends which may affect supplies** - keep an eye on factors such as raw materials cost/availability, competitor activity or changes to legislation which may affect the price or availability of supplies.

7. **Take action where there are likely to be problems or opportunities with supplies** - where your information suggests changes to supplies which may give you problems or opportunities, take, or recommend, appropriate action to turn the situation to your advantage.

8. **Keep complete and accurate records of negotiations and agreements with suppliers** - and pass this information on to appropriate people as soon as possible.

9. **Maintain goodwill** - throughout your negotiations with suppliers, make sure you retain their goodwill, and find mutually acceptable ways of settling any disputes.

Meeting Customer Needs

Maintaining a productive work environment

1. **Ensure the environment is as conducive to work as possible** - involve your staff in assessing the work environment to see if there are different ways it could be arranged to improve productivity.

2. **Ensure that conditions satisfy legal and organisational requirements** - check the relevant legislation and your internal guidelines, and make sure you have a safe work environment.

3. **Cater for special needs** - provide for any special needs of employees or potential employees to ensure they can work productively.

4. **Make sure equipment is properly maintained and used only by competent personnel** - regularly check all equipment in your area to see that it is properly maintained and that relevant staff have been trained to use it.

5. **Ensure you have a sufficient supply of resources** - plan what materials, equipment and resources you require to keep your operation running smoothly.

6. **Where you do not have sufficient resources, refer to the appropriate people** - let them know immediately if you are likely to run out of anything.

7. **Pass on recommendations for improving conditions** - where you identify opportunities for improving working conditions, let the appropriate people know right away, so the organisation can benefit as soon as possible.

8. **Report accidents and incidents promptly and accurately** - check that you, and your staff, are fully aware of the accident and hazard procedures and that they are followed at all times.

9. **Keep accurate records** - make sure your department's maintenance and health and safety records are accurate, legible and up-to-date.

Meeting Customer Needs

Meeting customer specifications

1. **Check that specifications are clear, complete and accurate** - where there is any omission or ambiguity, get clarification from your customer.
2. **Draw up plans and schedules to meet these specifications** - allow for contingencies in these plans.
3. **Brief all relevant people** - make sure they understand how the specifications, plans and schedules affect them.
4. **Monitor operations** - monitor what is happening and take appropriate action to ensure specifications are met.
5. **Make best use of resources** - use your human, capital and financial resources efficiently to meet the specifications.
6. **Encourage staff to take responsibility for meeting customer requirements** - involve staff in finding the best way to meet specifications and gain their commitment.
7. **Give staff feedback** - tell them how well they are doing in meeting customer requirements.
8. **Get feedback from customers** - use this feedback to improve future operations.
9. **Minimise disruptions to operations** - take appropriate action to reduce any factors which may disrupt operations.
10. **Take corrective action** - implement any changes without delay and inform relevant staff, colleagues and customers about these.
11. **Monitor corrective action** - make sure that changes are working, and use this experience to improve future operations.
12. **Keep complete and accurate records of operations** - keep records of activities and how well you met customer specifications and make these records available to appropriate people.

Meeting Customer Needs

Solving problems for customers

1. **Design systems to anticipate and avoid problems for customers** - design all your procedures to meet customer needs.

2. **Advise customers about your policies and procedures for solving their problems** - use appropriate media to publish your policies and procedures and alternative sources of assistance to which customers may refer.

3. **Identify and acknowledge the customer's perception of the problem** - where problems do occur, listen carefully in order to understand and acknowledge the customer's view of the problem.

4. **Gather all information relevant to the customer's problem** - refer to records and other people involved in order to get a full picture of the problem.

5. **Summarise the customer's problem** - summarise their perceptions and all other relevant information and check that the customer agrees with your summary of the problem.

6. **Keep the customer informed** - tell the customer how you plan to resolve the problem, how long it will take and give the customer progress reports where appropriate.

7. **Refer to organisational procedures** - examine and interpret procedures for handling customer complaints to identify a solution.

8. **Seek advice from colleagues or senior managers** - where organisational procedures do not offer a satisfactory solution ask colleagues for help in identifying alternative solutions.

9. **Implement the solution promptly** - once the solution has been identified, take prompt action to solve the customer's problem and inform the customer of the action taken.

10. **Monitor the delivery of the solution** - and make appropriate modifications to resolve any problems arising.

11. **Check customer's satisfaction** - where appropriate, check that the problem has been solved to the customer's satisfaction.

12. **Develop new procedures** - review the process and where policies or procedures do not offer a satisfactory solution, revise or develop new policies or procedures to avoid or address similar situations.

Managing Change

This section is about identifying, implementing and evaluating improvements.

The checklists will help you to:
- always be looking for areas where improvements can be made
- assess the benefits against any problems caused by the changes
- consult with all concerned to get them to agree to the changes
- implement your plans for change
- evaluate whether improvements have been achieved.

The process of *Managing Change* looks like this:

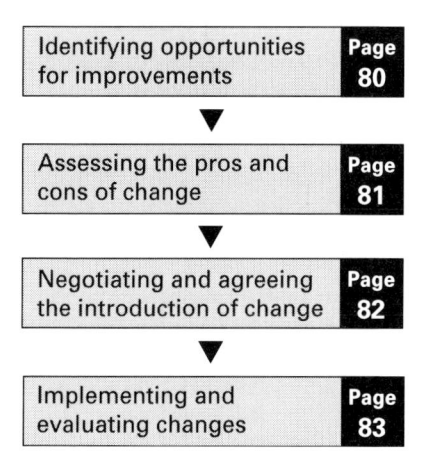

Identifying opportunities for improvements	Page 80

▼

Assessing the pros and cons of change	Page 81

▼

Negotiating and agreeing the introduction of change	Page 82

▼

Implementing and evaluating changes	Page 83

Refer to the checklists in the sections **Identifying and Evaluating Opportunities for Improvements** *(pages 17-19) and* **Supporting Continuous Improvement in Energy Usage** *(pages 40-51).*

Managing Change

Identifying opportunities for improvements

1. **Keep up to date with developments in your sector** - make sure you get relevant, valid, reliable information from various sources on developments in materials, equipment, technology and processes.

2. **Consider the importance of these developments to your organisation** - carry out a regular review of developments and analyse their significance to your organisation.

3. **Pass information on developments to the appropriate people** - if you think it is important, make sure your colleagues, staff and senior managers are aware of its significance.

4. **Identify opportunities for improvements** - use information on developments to identify opportunities for growth, improvements in procedures or improvements in quality.

5. **Monitor and evaluate your operations continuously** - always look for areas where improvements can be made and take appropriate action.

6. **Identify any obstacles to change** - take appropriate measures to alleviate any problems which may prevent improvements being made.

7. **Learn from your experience** - use your experience of previous improvements to help identify new ones.

Managing Change

Assessing the pros and cons of change

1. **Get complete and accurate information** - make sure you have sufficient, reliable information on both current and proposed services, products and systems to allow you to make a reliable assessment.

2. **Compare the advantages and disadvantages** - use qualitative and quantitative techniques to assess the pros and cons of current and proposed services, products and systems.

3. **Assess the implications of introducing changes** - changes may affect cashflow, working practices, staff morale, supply and distribution networks and customer loyalty; anticipate and assess the likely effect of changes.

4. **Take into account previous assessments of introducing change** - look at how realistic previous assessments turned out to be and use these to modify your current assessment.

5. **Present your recommendations to the appropriate people** - make your recommendations to senior managers or specialists in a way which helps them make a decision and in time to allow the decision to be put into effect.

6. **Amend your recommendations in the light of responses** - make appropriate alterations to your recommendations on the basis of the responses you get from senior managers and specialists.

Managing Change

Negotiating and agreeing the introduction of change

1. **Present information on projected change to the appropriate people** - let staff, colleagues, senior managers and others know about the changes at the earliest possible time, and in sufficient detail, to allow them to evaluate its impact on their area of responsibility.

2. **Conduct negotiations in a spirit of goodwill** - make sure you retain the support of others and find mutually acceptable ways of settling any disputes.

3. **Make compromises where appropriate** - it may be necessary to make compromises to accommodate other priorities, but make sure these compromises are consistent with your organisation's strategy, objectives and practices.

4. **Reach an agreement in line with your organisation's strategy** - and include detailed implementation plans.

5. **Keep records of negotiations and agreements** - make sure your records are complete and accurate and that they are available for others to refer to if necessary.

6. **Where you could not secure the changes you anticipated, tell your staff in a positive manner** - sometimes you are disappointed in not being able to obtain the changes you wanted for your team due to other organisational priorities; explain to your staff the reasons for this in a positive way.

7. **Encourage all relevant people to understand and participate in the changes** - communicate the changes and their effects to people, and gain their support.

Managing Change

Implementing and evaluating changes

1. **Present details of implementation plans to all concerned** - make sure that you brief everyone involved, or affected by, the changes on their role in the changes and the possible impact on their area.

2. **Encourage people to seek clarification** - check on their understanding of their role and encourage them to ask questions.

3. **Use resources in the most effective way** - plan carefully so that you meet the new requirements as cost-effectively as possible.

4. **Monitor the changes** - check to see that the changes have been implemented according to plan and that they result in the improvements anticipated.

5. **Evaluate the benefits of the changes** - compare the new way of working with the old; are the benefits as expected?

6. **Modify implementation plans and activities in the light of experience** - you may need to modify the way you implement changes to cope with unforeseen problems.

7. **Review the change process** - review the whole process of identifying, assessing, negotiating, agreeing, implementing and evaluating change, note ways of doing it better next time and make appropriate recommendations to senior managers, colleagues and specialists.

Managing the Operation

Quality Assurance

This section is about developing systems to ensure that you meet your customers needs on time, every time.

The checklist will help you to:
- be clear about your customers' needs
- involve staff and other colleagues in developing quality assurance systems
- monitor and publicise the benefits of quality assurance systems.

This section links closely with the sections on *Meeting Customer Needs* and *Managing Change*. It has just one checklist:

| Assuring quality | Page 86 |

Quality Assurance

Assuring quality

1. **Be clear about your customers' expectations and requirements** - quality is about fulfilling your customers' expectations on time, every time.

2. **Make recommendations for quality assurance systems to meet customers' expectations** - make sure your systems are in place to meet customer requirements, not to satisfy a bureaucratic whim.

3. **Encourage staff to help develop quality assurance systems** - consult the staff who are most involved with the operation to get their ideas and gain their commitment to following the quality assurance system.

4. **Present details of the quality assurance system, or modifications to it, to all those concerned** - make sure that you brief everyone involved or affected by the quality assurance system on their role or the possible impact on their area.

5. **Encourage people to seek clarification** - check on their understanding of their role and encourage them to ask questions.

6. **Make the best use of resources** - make sure your quality assurance system does not duplicate or add unnecessarily to the workload, but makes best use of existing procedures and activities.

7. **Publicise the benefits and results of quality assurance** - enhance employee commitment and customer satisfaction by making sure they are aware of the benefits that the quality assurance system is delivering.

8. **Monitor your quality assurance systems** - check whether they continue to deliver customer satisfaction and make any modifications required.

Time Management

This section is about making the most efficient use of your time.

The checklist will help you to:
- be clear about your objectives and your priorities
- plan your time and allow for contingencies
- delegate work where appropriate
- be decisive.

This section will help you with all other aspects of management. It has just one checklist:

| Managing your time | Page 88 |

Time Management

Managing your time

1. **Be clear about your objectives** - be clear about what you have to achieve, by when and what the priorities are.

2. **Identify what needs to be done to achieve these objectives** - identify what you, and others, need to do to achieve your objectives and estimate how long each activity will take.

3. **Plan your time** - plan these activities into your time on an annual, monthly, weekly and daily basis to ensure objectives are achieved on time; include time for evaluation.

4. **Delegate** - review your activities and, where possible, delegate those activities which could be done equally well by one of your staff, with training and guidance where appropriate.

5. **Handle paper once only** - when dealing with paper, decide immediately to respond, refer, file or destroy.

6. **Take decisions** - when faced with a choice, either make your choice or decide what further information you need to be able to make an informed choice.

7. **Control interruptions** - make it clear when you welcome consultation with others, and when you require uninterrupted time to complete an activity.

8. **Control digressions** - keep your objectives in mind and do not indulge in, or allow others to indulge in, digressions.

9. **Allow for contingencies** - allow time in your planning for additional activities or for activities to overrun.

10. **Review your activities** - review your progress towards your objectives on a regular basis and reschedule activities as necessary.

Managing People

Management is about meeting customer requirements with and through people. It involves:

Personnel Planning   91

   Planning human resource requirements   92
   Drawing up job specifications   93
   Assessing and selecting staff   94
   Making staff redundant   95

Developing Teams and Individuals   97

   Developing teams   98
   Developing individuals   99
   Developing yourself   100
   Coaching   101
   Mentoring   102
   Evaluating and improving training and development   103

Managing Teams and Individuals   105

   Planning work   106
   Allocating work   107
   Setting objectives   108
   Giving feedback   109

Working Relationships   111

   Building a relationship with your manager   112
   Building relationships with staff   113
   Building relationships with colleagues   114
   Minimising conflict   115

Managing Problems with Staff   117

   Counselling   118
   Implementing grievance and disciplinary procedures   119
   Firing staff   120

Equal Opportunities   121

   Promoting equal opportunities   122
   Encouraging diversity and fair working practices   123

Managing People

Personnel Planning

This section is about making sure you have the right people to do the jobs.

The checklists will help you to:
- be clear about the people you need to meet your organisational objectives
- specify the skills, qualities and attributes you are looking for in staff
- assess candidates against specific criteria and select those most appropriate
- make redundant those staff who are no longer required.

The process for *Personnel Planning* looks like this

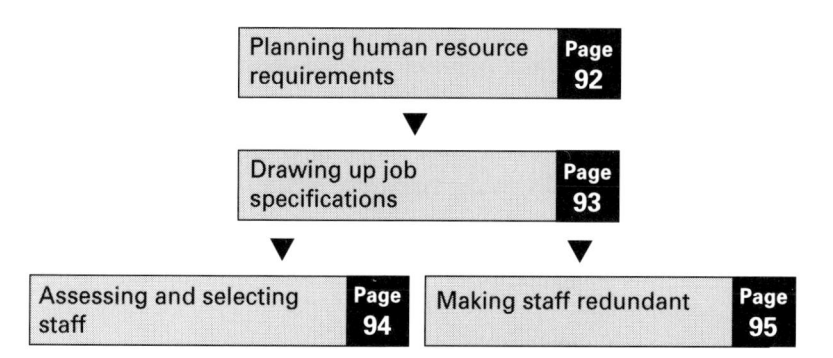

| Planning human resource requirements | Page 92 |

⬇

| Drawing up job specifications | Page 93 |

⬇   ⬇

| Assessing and selecting staff | Page 94 | | Making staff redundant | Page 95 |

Personnel Planning

Planning human resource requirements

1. **Identify the optimum human resources required to achieve objectives** - you will need people to help you achieve the objectives of your organisation, department, team or project; identify the number and type of staff needed to provide you with the best support at the most reasonable cost.

2. **Base your plans on current, valid and reliable information** - check your information is sound and up-to-date.

3. **Support your plans with appropriate calculations** - your estimates of the human resource required will need to be supported by calculations of the time required to complete tasks and the associated personnel costs, including training and development, and provision for special needs.

4. **Identify the skills and personal qualities required of the team and individuals** - look for a balance of strengths within the team.

5. **Be clear about organisational constraints** - specify where financial considerations, organisational policy or legal constraints affect your plans.

6. **Consult with colleagues and staff** - take into account the views of your colleagues, specialists and your staff on how best to meet your future human resource requirements.

7. **Present your plans on time and with the appropriate level of detail** - make sure your plans are accurate, contain sufficient detail for a decision to be made and are presented in time for you to take the necessary action.

Personnel Planning

Drawing up job specifications

1. **Be clear about the job role** - clearly state the purpose of the job and how it relates to organisational objectives and the team.

2. **Specify the job in sufficient detail** - think carefully about the job title, reporting relationships, key objectives and responsibilities and the terms and conditions of service.

3. **Specify the type of person required** - be clear about the knowledge, competences and qualities they will need.

4. **Consult with colleagues and staff** - take into account the views of your colleagues, specialists and your staff on the definition of the job and the skills, knowledge and qualities required.

5. **Check that the specification is clear, concise and complies with legal and organisational requirements** - consult with specialists if you are in doubt.

6. **Agree the specification with appropriate people** - check and agree the specification with colleagues, specialists and your staff before taking any action to recruit, transfer or change a person's job.

7. **Regularly review job specifications** - keep specifications under review to ensure that they still describe the job and meet the organisation's needs.

Personnel Planning

Assessing and selecting staff

1. **Check your organisation's procedures and legal requirements** - make sure that your process for assessing and selecting staff complies with your organisation's procedures and the law.

2. **Obtain, or draw up, criteria against which to judge candidates** - have clear, measurable criteria.

3. **Seek advice if you are not sure about any of the selection criteria** - consult with specialists if you are in doubt.

4. **Get sufficient information from candidates to be able to make a decision** - use a variety of appropriate assessment techniques, cv's, application forms, interviews, tests, references etc, to ensure you get all relevant information.

5. **Judge the information obtained against specified selection criteria** - you should be able to defend your decision to accept or reject a candidate by how well the candidates meet the selection criteria; do not let irrelevant factors affect your decision.

6. **Be fair and consistent** - correct any deviations from agreed procedures before you make your selection.

7. **Maintain confidentiality** - tell only authorised people of your selection recommendations.

8. **Keep clear, accurate and complete records** - you may need to refer back to them.

9. **Keep candidates informed** - tell candidates promptly and accurately of decisions following each stage of the selection process.

10. **Check that your choice is justifiable** - make sure you have selected the most suitable candidate from the evidence obtained and the process used; if in doubt, consult colleagues or specialists.

11. **Review the process and make appropriate recommendations for improvement** - consider every aspect of the process and make any recommendations for improving it, so that you and your colleagues can do better next time.

Personnel Planning

Making staff redundant

1. **Keep staff informed about current procedures** - ensure that staff are aware of your organisation's policy and any redundancy procedures, including appeals procedure.
2. **Avoid redundancies where possible** - accurate personnel planning will minimise the need for redundancies, but where these are inevitable explore alternatives such as early retirement or part-time working.
3. **Consult with staff** - consult with both individual staff and their representatives over the redundancy plan. Consultation will improve co-operation and may result in alternative, more acceptable approaches being adopted.
4. **Agree clear and fair selection criteria** - agree selection criteria which are unambiguous, can be clearly applied, are fair and comply with legal and organisational requirements.
5. **Apply selection criteria fairly and consistently** - consult with specialists if you are in doubt.
6. **Prepare to break the news** - rehearse what you will say to staff who will be made redundant, including responses to likely questions, and enlist the support of colleagues or specialists, as advised.
7. **Break the news quickly and compassionately** - tell staff quickly, clearly, confidentially and compassionately that they will be made redundant and what help is available to them.
8. **Offer alternative work** - where there are suitable jobs available, offer these alternatives with details of terms and conditions.
9. **Offer counselling** - offer staff appropriate counselling, resources, training and time off work to help them find another job and cope with the personal and practical implications of redundancy.
10. **Seek advice** - seek advice from colleagues and specialists, on all aspects of making staff redundant in order to ensure you comply with legal and organisational requirements.
11. **Keep staff and colleagues informed** - tell staff and colleagues about the redundancies and the reasons, without breaching confidentiality.
12. **Recommend any changes to policy or procedures** - tell the appropriate people of ways in which your organisation's policy or procedures could be improved.

Managing People

Developing Teams and Individuals

This section is about making sure your team has the skills to do their jobs.

The checklists will help you to:
- develop a balanced team with all the skills needed
- help individuals identify and develop the skills they need
- develop the skills you need for your job
- coach individuals to develop new skills
- be an adviser or mentor to individuals to help them develop
- evaluate and improve the training and development processes.

The process for *Developing Teams and Individuals* looks like this:

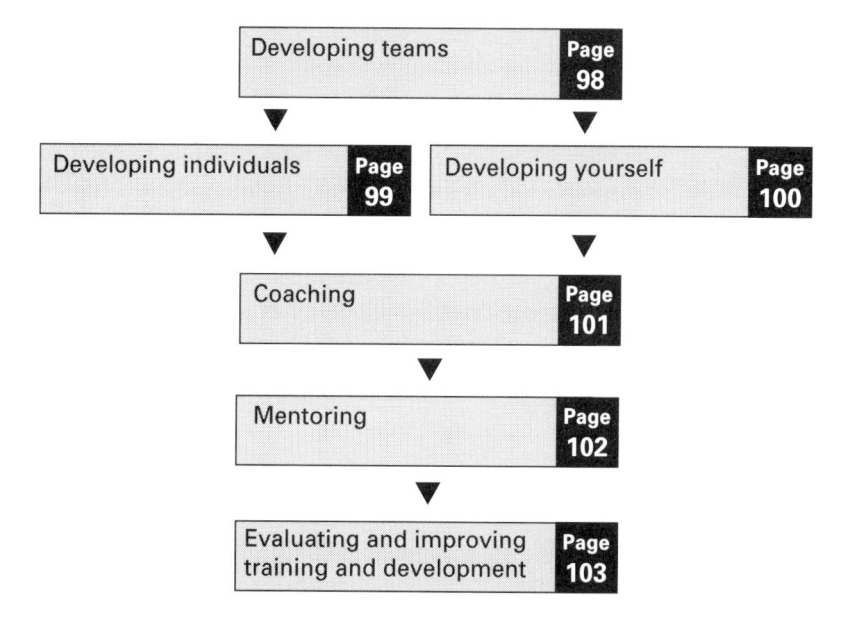

| Developing teams | **Page 98** |

▼ ▼

| Developing individuals | **Page 99** | | Developing yourself | **Page 100** |

▼

| Coaching | **Page 101** |

▼

| Mentoring | **Page 102** |

▼

| Evaluating and improving training and development | **Page 103** |

Refer also to the checklists in the section **Encouraging Commitment to Energy Efficiency** *(pages 35-38).*

Developing Teams and Individuals

Developing teams

1. **Involve all team members in evaluating the team's development needs** - get them involved in identifying their own strengths and weaknesses.

2. **Assess the team's strengths and weaknesses** - looking at each individual and at the team as a whole, assess and acknowledge the team's strengths and weaknesses to carry out current and future work.

3. **Consult with all team members on how to meet development needs** - gain the team's commitment by involving them in planning how to meet development needs.

4. **Be clear about the objectives of development plans** - your objectives should be clear, relevant and realistic for individuals and the team as a whole.

5. **Optimise the use of resources** - when planning development activities, use available resources effectively.

6. **Minimise unproductive friction** - be clear about individuals' responsibilities in the team to minimise risk of bad feeling.

7. **Regularly review your plans** - discuss and agree improvements to development plans with team members, other colleagues and specialists at appropriate intervals.

Developing Teams and Individuals

Developing individuals

1. **Involve individuals in identifying their own development needs** - get them to identify their own strengths and weaknesses.

2. **Discuss development needs and plans with individuals** - gain their commitment by involving individuals in planning how to meet their development needs.

3. **Be clear about the objectives of development plans** - your objectives should be clear, relevant and realistic for the individual.

4. **Balance business needs with individual aspirations** - plans should help individuals to develop the skills they need to do their current job and meet future job requirements and career aspirations.

5. **Optimise the use of resources** - when planning development activities, use available resources effectively.

6. **Regularly review your plans** - regularly discuss and agree improvements to development plans with individuals, other colleagues and specialists.

Developing Teams and Individuals

Developing yourself

1. **Take responsibility for developing yourself** - ensure you develop the skills you need to achieve your objectives.

2. **Identify your own strengths and weaknesses** - measure your current skills as a manager against appropriate standards and by getting feedback from your line manager, colleagues and staff.

3. **Set yourself clear development objectives** - make your objectives achievable, realistic and challenging.

4. **Consider the needs of the organisation** - include objectives to develop as a team member.

5. **Allow sufficient time and resources** - allocate sufficient time and appropriate resources to achieve your development objectives.

6. **Regularly review progress and performance** - check your progress against your objectives with your line manager and specialists at regular intervals and revise your plan as appropriate.

7. **Compare feedback with your own perceptions of your performance** - compare feedback from your line manager, colleagues, staff and others with how well you think you are doing; and improve your future performance as a result.

Developing Teams and Individuals

Coaching

1. **Identify the individual's development needs** - use appropriate methods to assess the needs of the person you are coaching.
2. **Agree learning objectives** - discuss and agree with the individual the learning objectives to be achieved.
3. **Take account of the individual** - design your coaching to match the individual's learning preferences, and deliver the coaching in a manner and at a pace appropriate to the learner.
4. **Analyse the components of skills** - make sure you understand the different components of the skill and convey these in the sequence in which they need to be learnt.
5. **Identify inhibiting factors** - clearly identify and discuss with learners any factors which are inhibiting their learning.
6. **Check learners' progress** - check regularly on progress and modify coaching as appropriate.
7. **Give feedback** - provide timely feedback to learners on the process of learning and on their progress towards learning objectives in a positive and encouraging manner.
8. **Receive feedback** - ask learners how they feel about the process of learning and their speed of progress and modify coaching as appropriate.

Developing Teams and Individuals

Mentoring

1. **Identify the individual's learning objectives** - discuss and identify the learning objectives to be achieved with individual mentees, their line managers and others involved.

2. **Agree the support mentees require** - specify and agree the roles, responsibilities and resources needed to help mentees achieve their learning objectives.

3. **Identify and overcome any difficulties in obtaining this support** - identify likely difficulties in obtaining the necessary people and resources and agree ways of overcoming these difficulties.

4. **Develop effective working relationships** - both with mentees and with others who can provide support.

5. **Provide guidance** - provide accurate, timely and appropriate advice and guidance on learning methods and opportunities, and on other sources of information and advice.

6. **Encourage independent decision-making** - provide guidance in a way which encourages mentees to take responsibility for their own development and enables them to make informed decisions.

7. **Facilitate learning and assessment opportunities** - identify and facilitate opportunities for mentees to develop, practice, apply and assess new skills, knowledge and experience in a structured way.

8. **Provide on-going support** - within the agreed role, provide mentees with support for their learning, development and assessment, as required.

9. **Give feedback** - provide timely feedback to mentees on their progress towards learning objectives in a positive and encouraging manner.

10. **Review the mentoring process** - at appropriate intervals, discuss the mentoring process and your relationship with mentees and modify as appropriate.

Developing Teams and Individuals

Evaluating and improving training and development

1. **Identify clearly the training and development objectives** - be clear what the objectives are and how to measure whether they have been achieved.

2. **Debrief the learners** - discuss with individuals and teams involved in training and development how useful it was, how satisfied they were with its delivery and how well it will apply to their work.

3. **Find suitable alternatives where training and development did not meet the needs** - discuss and agree with the individuals and teams concerned alternative training and development which may be more appropriate.

4. **Modify team and individual training and development plans** - where plans were unrealistic, discuss and agree modified plans with the teams and individuals concerned.

5. **Check whether objectives have been achieved** - apply the agreed measures to see to what extent objectives have been achieved.

6. **Pass on your experience** - discuss the strengths and weaknesses of the training and development processes used with specialists, your line manager and colleagues so they can gain from your experience.

7. **Benefit from your experience** - use your experience of training and development processes to help you identify more appropriate training and development in the future.

Managing People

Managing Teams and Individuals

This section is about making sure your team get the job done.

The checklists will help you to:
- plan the work to meet your objectives
- allocate work amongst the team
- set clear objectives for each member of the team
- evaluate performance and provide feedback to staff.

The process for *Managing Teams and Individuals* looks like this:

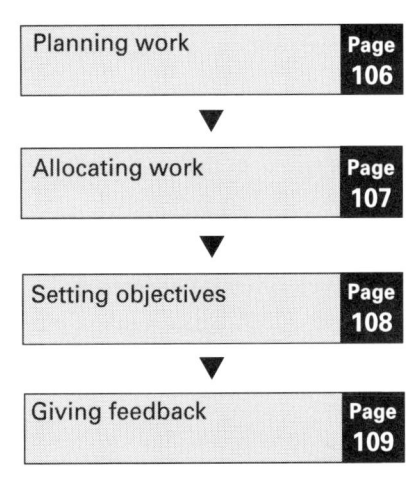

Planning work	Page 106

▼

Allocating work	Page 107

▼

Setting objectives	Page 108

▼

Giving feedback	Page 109

Managing Teams and Individuals

Planning work

1. **Plan work in order to meet organisational objectives** - make sure your plans are consistent with team and organisational objectives.

2. **Assess the degree of direction required by each member of staff** - inexperienced or less confident staff may need far more direction and help in planning their work than more experienced and self-assured colleagues.

3. **Encourage individuals to contribute to planning work activities and methods** - the staff who will be carrying out the work are likely to have sound ideas as to the most efficient ways of doing it.

4. **Include staff suggestions on working methods, resources and time required** - this will help to ensure their commitment to the work.

5. **Select work methods and activities which meet both operational and developmental objectives** - choose work methods and activities which balance management priorities, organisational objectives, legal requirements and opportunities for individual development.

6. **Select cost-effective work methods** - choose work methods which make the best use of available material, capital and people.

7. **Seek advice where legal requirements and organisational/developmental objectives conflict** - consult with your line manager, specialists or external advisers.

Managing Teams and Individuals

Allocating work

1. **Allocate work according to availability of resources and skills of staff** - optimise the resources and the skills of the staff available to meet organisational objectives.
2. **Clearly define team and individual responsibilities and limits of authority** - make sure staff understand their own responsibilities and limits of authority, and those with whom they work closely, in order to avoid possible conflict, duplication or omission of important responsibilities.
3. **Provide learning and developmental opportunities for staff within the work allocated** - take opportunities to develop new skills which staff will need in the future.
4. **Brief staff on their work in a manner and at a level and pace which is appropriate** - inexperienced or less confident staff may need a more detailed briefing on their responsibilities and work than their more experienced and self-assured colleagues.
5. **Encourage staff to seek clarification** - check on their understanding and give them opportunities to ask questions.
6. **Provide access to people who can help them meet their objectives** - staff may need access to colleagues, managers, specialists and external advisers to help them meet their work and developmental objectives.
7. **Provide the right level of supervision** - some staff will require much closer supervision than others.
8. **Ensure that work allocations are realistic** - carefully calculate the time, cost and criticality of the work to ensure appropriate resources have been allocated.
9. **Reallocate work where appropriate** - if the way work was allocated proves to be unrealistic, or organisational demands change, reallocate work whilst minimising any detrimental impact on time or cost.
10. **Benefit from your experience** - evaluate how well you have allocated work in order to improve your performance in the future.

Managing Teams and Individuals

Setting objectives

1. **Involve staff in setting objectives** - ask staff to be proactive in identifying what their objectives should be.

2. **Set clear objectives** - agree SMART objectives with your staff which are:
   Specific   - be precise about what must be achieved
   Measurable - how will you know if it has been achieved?
   Agreed   - by you, the member of staff and the team
   Realistic   - objectives have to be achievable
   Time-bound - to be completed by a specified time.

3. **Explain objectives clearly** - when explaining objectives, think about the person you are talking to, and make sure you communicate with them in a manner and at a pace which is appropriate.

4. **Encourage staff to seek clarification** - check on their understanding and give them opportunities to ask questions.

5. **Update objectives regularly** - review objectives as often as appropriate in the light of changes to individual and team workloads and organisational priorities.

6. **Check that objectives have been achieved** - as part of the objective-setting process, agree the date when you will review with your staff whether the objectives have been achieved.

7. **Provide feedback** - both formally and informally which includes constructive suggestions and encouragement for improving future performance.

Managing Teams and Individuals

Giving feedback

1. **Seek opportunities to provide feedback to teams and individuals on their performance** - feedback helps people to understand if they are doing a good job or if there are areas in which they can improve. Feedback can be given formally or informally, orally or in writing.

2. **Choose an appropriate time and place to give the feedback** - feedback is more useful and relevant if provided quickly. Sometimes it is appropriate to give feedback publicly, but often a quiet word with a member of staff is what is required.

3. **Recognise good performance and achievement** - take opportunities to congratulate staff on their successes.

4. **Provide constructive suggestions and encouragement for improving future performance** - when staff are not performing well, tell them, and advise them how they can improve.

5. **Encourage staff to contribute to their own assessment** - ask open-ended questions about how they view their performance and invite them to be specific.

6. **Provide feedback in sufficient detail and in a manner and at a level and pace which is appropriate to the staff concerned** - some staff may readily understand your feedback on their performance, with others it may be necessary to be very specific about their performance and any improvements required.

7. **Encourage staff to seek clarification** - check their understanding and give them the opportunity to ask questions.

8. **Encourage staff to make suggestions on how systems/procedures could be improved** - their performance may be greatly enhanced by changes to procedures and working practices.

9. **Record details of any action agreed** - make a note of actions agreed to maintain or improve their performance or change procedures, and inform the appropriate people.

10. **Review performance** - check back at an appropriate point to see whether performance has improved or been maintained.

Working Relationships

This section is about building effective working relationships with all those you work with.

The checklists will help you to:
- take time to build effective working relationships
- consult with colleagues and keep them informed
- be honest and open with people
- provide support and keep your promises
- take steps to minimise any possible conflicts.

The process of building effective *Working Relationships* looks like this

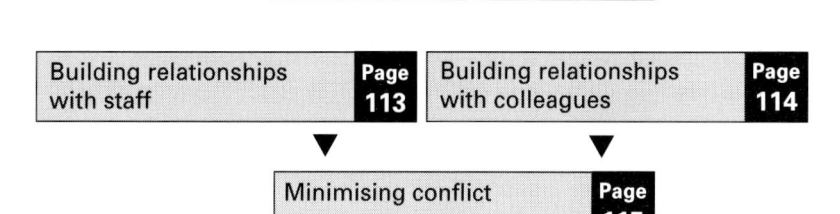

| Building a relationship with your manager | Page 112 |

| Building relationships with staff | Page 113 | | Building relationships with colleagues | Page 114 |

| Minimising conflict | Page 115 |

Working Relationships

Building a relationship with your manager

1. **Keep your manager informed** - provide an appropriate level of detail about activities, progress, results and achievements.
2. **Provide information about emerging threats and opportunities** - let your manager know about possible threats and opportunities clearly, accurately and with the appropriate level of urgency.
3. **Seek information and advice** - ask your manager for information and advice on policy and ways of working whenever appropriate.
4. **Present clear proposals for action** - present proposals at the appropriate time and with the right level of detail. Your manager will require more detail the greater the degree of change, expenditure and risk involved in your proposal.
5. **Identify the reasons why a proposal has been rejected** - try to find out clearly what the reasons are and, if appropriate, put forward alternative proposals.
6. **Make efforts to maintain a good relationship with your manager** - even if you do have disagreements, try to prevent these damaging your relationship.
7. **Meet your objectives** - always try to fulfil the objectives agreed with your manager in full; where circumstances prevent you from meeting objectives, inform your manager at the earliest possible time.
8. **Support your manager** - give your manager your backing, especially in situations which involve people outside your team.
9. **Be open and direct** - discuss any concerns about the relationship with your manager directly with him or her.

Working Relationships

Building relationships with staff

1. **Take time to build honest and constructive relationships with staff** - get to know your staff and allow them to get to know you.

2. **Keep staff informed** - provide them with relevant information on organisational policy and strategy, progress, emerging threats and opportunities.

3. **Consult staff about proposed activities** - give them the opportunity to state their views so they can be taken into account.

4. **Encourage staff to offer their ideas and views** - use open questions to get their contributions.

5. **Give recognition for their ideas and views** - thank them and show the value you place on their ideas.

6. **Give clear reasons where ideas are not taken up** - where it is not possible to take up a good idea, acknowledge the value of the idea and explain why it is not possible to adopt it.

7. **Encourage staff to seek clarification** - check their understanding and give them the opportunity to ask questions.

8. **Keep your promises** - when you make promises and undertakings to staff, make sure they are realistic and that you honour them.

9. **Support your staff** - give staff your backing especially in situations which involve people outside your team.

10. **Be open and direct** - discuss concerns about the quality of work directly with the member of staff concerned.

Working Relationships

Building relationships with colleagues

1. **Take time to build honest and constructive relationships with colleagues** - get to know your colleagues and allow them to get to know you.

2. **Encourage open, honest and friendly behaviour** - ask open questions to get their opinions.

3. **Share information and opinions with colleagues** - stop and think who could benefit from any information or idea you have.

4. **Offer help and advice with sensitivity** - you can often help a colleague or provide advice on a difficult problem.

5. **Deal courteously with colleagues when you have differences of opinion** - you will not always agree with colleagues; discuss these different views respectfully and try to understand them.

6. **Resolve conflicts amicably** - always maintain mutual respect.

7. **Keep your promises** - when you make promises to colleagues, make sure they are realistic and that you honour them.

Working Relationships

Minimising conflict

1. **Explain to staff the standards of work and behaviour you expect** - some staff will readily appreciate the standards you and your organisation require; others may require a fuller and more detailed explanation.

2. **Clearly allocate work and responsibilities** - you can greatly reduce the potential for conflict by making sure your staff are clear about the responsibilities of each member of the team.

3. **Encourage staff to discuss problems which affect their work** - make it clear that you are available to help resolve these problems.

4. **Quickly identify potential or actual conflicts between staff** - when conflicts appear, or are likely, involve the relevant staff in identifying the nature and cause of the conflict early on.

5. **Take prompt action to resolve conflicts** - do not let the conflict fester, but take decisive action to deal with it.

6. **Ensure solutions satisfy legal and organisational requirements** - check that you are not infringing any legislation or procedures and that your solution helps meet organisational objectives.

7. **Keep accurate and complete records of the conflict** - particularly where the conflict is serious, keep notes of what happened and what was agreed, in case there is any comeback.

8. **Monitor the situation** - keep an eye on the situation to ensure that the conflict does not reappear.

9. **Learn from your experience** - use the experience to help you, and your staff, avoid or quickly resolve conflicts in the future.

Managing People

Managing Problems with Staff

This section is about ensuring the best outcome when you have problems with staff.

The checklists will help you to:
- counsel staff when personal matters are affecting their work
- action grievance and disciplinary procedures
- dismiss staff, where this is the most appropriate option.

This section covers:

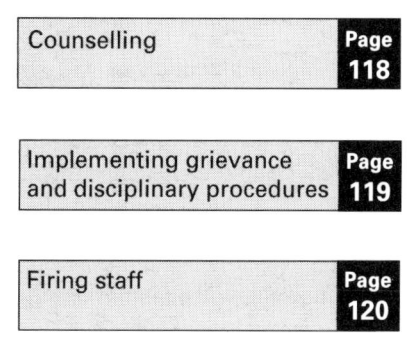

| Counselling | Page 118 |

| Implementing grievance and disciplinary procedures | Page 119 |

| Firing staff | Page 120 |

Managing Problems with Staff

Counselling

1. **Identify the need for counselling quickly** - be alert to the need to counsel staff; changes in mood, a fall-off in performance, stress symptoms, or a word from a colleague may indicate the need to counsel staff.

2. **Choose an appropriate time and place** - counselling on personal matters affecting an individual's work needs to take place in a private place and at a time which allows for full discussion without interruptions.

3. **Follow your organisation's guidelines or personnel policies** - if your organisation has specified personnel policies, check to make sure you follow these.

4. **Encourage the individual to discuss the situation fully** - help the individual to understand the situation and all the factors which affect it.

5. **Encourage the individual to take responsibility for their own decisions and actions** - remember you are helping them to solve a problem, you are not solving it for them.

6. **Recommend an appropriate counselling service where appropriate** - when you do not have the skills or knowledge to help the individual, recommend they see a specialist in your organisation or an external counselling service, doctor etc.

7. **Monitor the situation** - keep an eye on the situation and offer further counselling sessions if these are necessary.

Managing Problems with Staff

Implementing grievance and disciplinary procedures

1. **Keep staff informed about current procedures** - make sure they have up-to-date copies of your organisation's grievance and disciplinary procedures and remind them of these from time to time.

2. **Action grievance and disciplinary procedures with minimum delay** - act promptly to prevent the situation getting out of hand and causing damage to the organisation or the staff concerned.

3. **Act in accordance with legal and organisational requirements** - check, with a specialist if necessary, both the legal situation and your organisation's procedures.

4. **Ask for advice** - where appropriate, confidentially ask a specialist, your line manager or colleagues for advice on how to deal effectively with these difficult situations, especially where legal and organisational requirements conflict.

5. **Involve a third party** - where appropriate, ask a third party - specialist, line manager or colleague - to become involved to ensure you implement the procedures fairly and impartially.

6. **Be, and be seen to be, impartial** - get all the facts of the case before you and make decisions which are objective and can be shown to be free of personal bias.

7. **Keep accurate and complete records** - make detailed notes of the whole proceedings and, where appropriate, copy these to the member(s) of staff concerned and specialists.

8. **Monitor the situation** - keep an eye on the situation to ensure that the problems which led to the implementation of grievance or disciplinary procedures do not reappear.

9. **Learn from your experience** - use the experience to help you, and your staff, avoid or quickly resolve the problems in the future.

10. **Recommend any improvements to the procedures** - tell the appropriate people of any ways in which the procedures could be improved.

Managing Problems with Staff

Firing staff

1. **Avoid the need to fire staff wherever possible** - good recruitment and selection, training, development and counselling techniques will minimise the need to fire staff.

2. **Follow disciplinary procedures** - make sure you follow your organisation's disciplinary procedures in detail.

3. **Seek advice** - seek advice from colleagues and specialists, inside or outside your organisation, on all aspects of firing staff in order to ensure you comply with legal and organisational requirements.

4. **Involve a third party** - where appropriate, ask a third party - specialist, line manager or colleague - to become involved to ensure you follow procedures fairly and impartially.

5. **Get the facts** - make sure you get all information relevant to the dismissal. If necessary, suspend the member of staff on full pay until you have all the facts available.

6. **Prepare to break the news** - rehearse what you will say to the member of staff, including responses to likely questions, and enlist the support of colleagues or specialists as appropriate.

7. **Give clear, fair grounds for dismissal** - check that your reasons for dismissing the member of staff are clear and fair grounds for dismissal, and give these both orally and in writing.

8. **Summarily dismiss staff in the case of gross misconduct** - dismiss staff without notice or pay in lieu of notice in the event of gross misconduct. When in doubt, suspend on full pay until you can consult specialists or gather all the facts.

9. **Keep staff and colleagues informed** - tell staff and colleagues about the dismissal and the reasons, without breaching confidentiality.

10. **Review the procedures and reasons for dismissal** - tell the appropriate people of any ways in which the procedures could be improved or future dismissals avoided.

Equal Opportunities

This section is about providing equal working opportunities, encouraging diversity and discouraging unfair discrimination.

The checklists will help you to:
- develop, implement and evaluate your equal opportunities policy and action plan
- encourage staff to use a range of appropriate working styles
- promote fair working practices.

The process of managing *Equal Opportunities* looks like this:

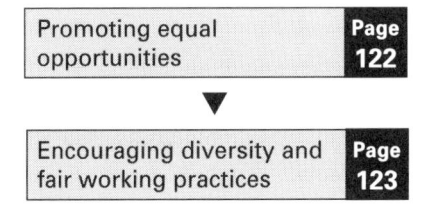

Promoting equal opportunities	Page 122

▼

Encouraging diversity and fair working practices	Page 123

Equal Opportunities

Promoting equal opportunities

1. **Contribute to the development of your organisation's equal opportunities policy** - offer your views and recommendations on how the policy should be developed.

2. **Involve staff, colleagues and customers** - encourage them to help develop your equal opportunities action plan, identify areas where opportunities are unfairly restricted and gain their commitment to the plan.

3. **Agree measures** - specify the criteria by which you can assess progress in your action plan.

4. **Collect and analyse information** - find out whether some groups of potential customers are excluded from obtaining your services or products; check whether certain employees, or potential employees, are denied access to development, employment or promotion opportunities.

5. **Identify the strengths of all employees** - especially those from under-represented groups, and identify how these strengths can contribute to your organisation's objectives.

6. **Identify special needs** - identify any special needs of customers, potential customers, employees or potential employees.

7. **Publish your action plan** - including actions to meet special needs and address any imbalances, as well as taking positive action to support under-represented groups.

8. **Communicate action plan to staff** - make sure staff are aware of their responsibilities and duties within the equal opportunities policy and action plan.

9. **Provide training and development opportunities** - provide appropriate training and development to help staff fulfil their duties in the action plan.

10. **Implement your action plan and evaluate your performance** - use agreed measures to monitor your progress against the action plan and modify the plan as appropriate.

Equal Opportunities

Encouraging diversity and fair working practices

1. **Communicate your equal opportunities policy to staff** - make sure staff are aware of the standards of behaviour expected of them and the consequences of unacceptable behaviour.

2. **Encourage a diversity of working styles** - encourage staff to develop a repertoire of appropriate working styles.

3. **Support natural working styles and behaviour** - encourage staff to use their natural and preferred working style and behaviour as long as they are consistent with the achievement of your organisational objectives.

4. **Discourage stereotyping** - discourage staff from imposing stereotypes and styles of working which are inconsistent with individuals' backgrounds.

5. **Discourage rigid approaches** - where particular styles of working are inhibited without good work-related reasons, provide feedback and suggestions to encourage more diverse approaches.

6. **Give feedback and suggestions sensitively** - where the style of working is inhibiting achievement of objectives, give feedback and suggestions to individuals in ways which are sensitive to their racial, social, gender or physical circumstances.

7. **Challenge discriminatory behaviour** - clearly explain the problems this behaviour may cause and the sanctions which will be applied if it continues.

8. **Implement disciplinary procedures** - take prompt action where unfair discriminatory behaviour persists.

9. **Seek guidance and support** - where you are unsure of the effect of your own, a member of your staff's or a colleague's behaviour on another person, seek guidance and support from specialists, inside or outside your organisation.

Managing People

Managing Finance

Managing Finance is about establishing and agreeing budgets for providing services to customers, and ensuring that costs are kept to a minimum. It involves:

Managing Budgets 127

    Preparing budgets 128
    Negotiating and agreeing budgets 129
    Monitoring budgets 130

Cost Control 131

    Controlling costs 132

Managing Finance

Managing Budgets

This section is about making sure projects and operations meet their financial targets.

The checklists will help you to:
- prepare estimates of income and expenditure based on the best information available
- negotiate effectively with those who have to agree the budget
- regularly check on performance against budget and make modifications where appropriate.

The process for *Managing Budgets* looks like this:

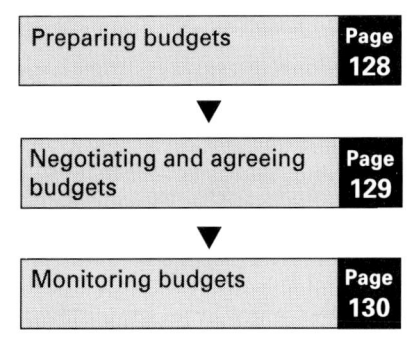

Preparing budgets	Page 128

▼

Negotiating and agreeing budgets	Page 129

▼

Monitoring budgets	Page 130

Managing Budgets

Preparing budgets

1. **Prepare accurate estimates of benefits, income and costs** - base your estimates on valid, reliable information, with historical data and trends where available.

2. **Assess alternative courses of action** - before submitting your budget and recommending expenditure assess the relative benefits and costs of alternative courses of action.

3. **Encourage staff to contribute to the budget** - if staff are involved in the process of drawing up the budget, they will be more committed to achieving the benefits and income and keeping within agreed costs.

4. **Clearly indicate the benefits over time** - be sure to specify what will be the net benefit from the expenditure.

5. **State your assumptions** - make it clear what assumptions you have made and why.

6. **Allow for contingencies** - take into account future changes which may affect the level of income and expenditure.

7. **Check your budgets with others** - where other people have been involved in providing information or making suggestions, check the details with them before submitting your final budget.

8. **Present your budget clearly and concisely** - make use of any forms which your organisation may have developed for presenting budgets.

9. **Be prepared to give a fuller explanation** - have all your information and arguments to hand to counter any challenges to your proposed budget.

10. **Learn from your experience** - compare actual costs and benefits with the budget and use this information to help you improve your budgeting in the future.

Managing Budgets

Negotiating and agreeing budgets

1. **Prepare people in advance** - involve your staff, colleagues and those who will be agreeing the budgets in discussing assumptions and drawing up the budgets.

2. **State your assumptions and the contingencies allowed for** - make it clear what assumptions you have made and what contingencies you have anticipated.

3. **Present your budget clearly and concisely** - emphasise the benefits making use of any forms the organisation may have developed for presenting budgets.

4. **Be as accurate as you can in your estimates** - use all the information available to support your calculations.

5. **Allow sufficient time for negotiation** - present your budget sufficiently early to allow you to provide further information if required.

6. **Negotiate with a spirit of good-will** - show that you intend to find a mutually acceptable solution.

7. **Seek clarification where there is uncertainty or disagreement** - ask for guidance and help in finding a mutually acceptable solution.

8. **Publish the budget decisions** - tell all those concerned about the outcomes of budget negotiations promptly, in order to secure their support, co-operation and confidence.

Managing Budgets

Monitoring budgets

1. **Keep expenditure within agreed limits** - be clear what your budget limits are, make sure you keep within these and check that all expenditure conforms to your organisation's policies and procedures.

2. **Phase expenditure according to a planned time-scale** - make sure you do not overspend your budget in any period, even if you are still within budget for the year, as this will be detrimental to cashflow.

3. **Check actual income and expenditure against budgets** - get accurate information on sales and costs at appropriate intervals.

4. **Report any likely over or underspend against budget** - let the appropriate people know as soon as possible of any potential variance against budget.

5. **Report any likely variance in income against budget** - let the appropriate people know as soon as possible if income is likely to be under or over budget.

6. **Give the reasons for any variances** - analyse the causes for variances in income or expenditure and propose corrective action.

7. **Take prompt corrective action** - take appropriate action where there are actual or potential significant deviations from budget.

8. **Get authority for changes in allocations between budget heads** - where you need to spend more in one budget head and less in another, obtain any necessary authorisation from the appropriate people.

9. **Get approval for changes to budgets** - where you need to change your budget during the accounting period, get appproval from the appropriate people.

Cost Control

This section is about ensuring everybody is continuously looking for ways of controlling or reducing costs.

The checklist will help you to:

- make your team aware how they can help control costs
- keep tight control on expenditure
- take prompt corrective action where expenditure looks like getting out of control.

This section links closely with *Managing Budgets* and *Managing Change*. It has just one checklist:

Controlling costs	Page 132

Cost Control

Controlling costs

1. **Make every member of your team aware of how they can help to control costs** - get them to consider areas where costs could be reduced and bring to their attention costs they could help to reduce.

2. **Keep expenditure within agreed budgets** - know what your budget limits are and check that you keep within them.

3. **Where expenditure is outside your responsibility, refer requests promptly to the appropriate people** - many costs are the responsibility of another department; let them know promptly if you need their authorisation for expenditure.

4. **Keep records of expenditure** - keep accurate and complete records available for reference.

5. **Carefully assess information on costs and the use of resources** - regular reviews of costs will help you identify areas where these can be reduced or resources better utilised.

6. **Look for improvements** - make recommendations for efficiency improvements as quickly as possible to the appropriate people.

7. **Take prompt corrective action** - where expenditure is likely to exceed budget, report this immediately to the appropriate people and take action to minimise the effects.

Managing Information

Managing Information is about ensuring prompt access to information in order to make decisions. It involves:

Using Information	**135**
Obtaining and evaluating information	136
Recording and storing information	137
Forecasting trends and developments	138
Presenting information and advice	139
Meetings	**141**
Leading meetings	142
Participating in meetings	143

Operational Management

Using Information

This section is about obtaining, using and presenting information to aid decision-making.

The checklists will help you to:

- identify and obtain the information you need
- record and store information in a way which makes it easy to retrieve
- evaluate the value of information
- use information to forecast future trends and developments
- present information and provide advice to others.

The process of *Using Information* looks like this:

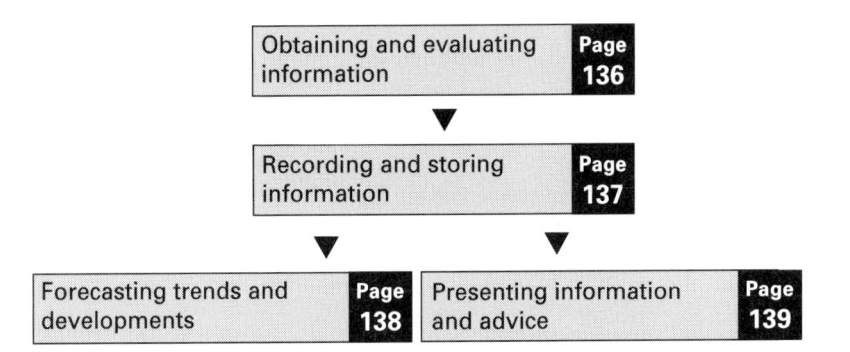

Obtaining and evaluating information	Page 136

▼

Recording and storing information	Page 137

▼   ▼

Forecasting trends and developments	Page 138	Presenting information and advice	Page 139

Refer also to the Energy Management section, particularly to the checklists in the sections **Providing Advice on Energy Strategies** *(pages 21-23),* **Promoting the Efficient Use of Energy** *(pages 31-33) and* **Supporting Energy Efficiency** *(pages 39-51).*

Using Information

Obtaining and evaluating information

1. **Identify what information you require** - regularly consider the kind of information you are going to need.

2. **Review your sources of information** - regularly review a wide range of sources of information and consider how useful, reliable and cost-effective they are.

3. **Develop your networks** - establish, maintain and develop contacts with people who may be able to provide you with useful information.

4. **Seek out all relevant information** - make sure you have information on all relevant factors affecting current or potential operations.

5. **Try alternative ways of getting information** - if you are having trouble getting information from one source, try a different route in, or an alternative source.

6. **Collect information in time for it to be of use** - make sure information arrives before the deadline.

7. **Present information in a suitable form to aid decision-making** - use summaries, diagrams and recommendations to help decision-making.

8. **Draw appropriate conclusions** - make sure your conclusions are fully supported by the relevant information and reasoned argument.

9. **Review your methods of obtaining information** - review your methods on a regular basis and improve them where necessary.

Using Information

Recording and storing information

1. **Record information accurately** - check the quality of records.

2. **Record information in appropriate detail** - you will need to keep a different level of detail on information, depending on how significant it is and how you anticipate using it.

3. **Record and store information using accepted formats, systems and procedures** - your organisation may have developed formal procedures and systems for storing different types of information, both paper-based and on computer.

4. **Make sure you can retrieve information promptly when required** - consider how urgently the information may be needed.

5. **Review your methods for recording and storing information** - re-evaluate your methods, systems and procedures on a regular basis to check that they are as effective and efficient as possible.

6. **Introduce new methods of recording and storing information as needed** - regularly review whether the supply of information continues to meet requirements.

7. **Analyse and correct any breakdowns in the methods of recording and storing information** - when systems do breakdown, analyse the cause, and take action to ensure similar breakdowns do not re-occur.

8. **Comply with legal requirements** - ensure your systems for recording, storing and providing information meet legal requirements.

Using Information

Forecasting trends and developments

1. **Base your forecasts on the best information available** - make sure you are using the best information given the constraints of time and cost.

2. **Make your forecasts of trends and developments at an appropriate time** - you will need to make some forecasts prior to planning; other developments may require forecasts to be regularly updated.

3. **Provide suitable quantitative information for decision making** - include in your forecasts sufficient quantitative information to allow you, and your colleagues, to be able to make decisions about allocating resources.

4. **State the assumptions underlying your forecasts** - clearly state your assumptions and the reasons for them.

5. **Clearly state the degree of certainty of your forecasts** - highlight those areas which are most at risk or where there is little evidence to support your forecast.

6. **Clearly illustrate the impact of trends and developments** - show how these trends will affect operations and the achievement of organisational objectives.

7. **Review your forecasts** - analyse the reasons for any inaccuracies in your forecasts, and use this information to improve future forecasts.

Using Information

Presenting information and advice

1. **Communicate** - seize opportunities to disseminate information and advice.

2. **Make sure your information is current, relevant and accurate** - prepare carefully what you are going to say and check it with colleagues or specialists.

3. **Check that your advice is consistent with organisational policy** - check with colleagues or specialists to ensure you are providing accurate advice.

4. **Support your advice** - where appropriate, provide reasoned argument and evidence to support your advice.

5. **Think about your audience** - put yourself in your audience's position, think what information they need, and present it in a manner, and at a level and pace which is appropriate.

6. **Check that your audience has understood** - ask questions, or use feedback, to check your audience has understood the information presented.

Meetings

This section is about leading and participating in meetings to make decisions.

The checklists will help you to:
- be clear about the purpose of the meeting and make sure its objectives are achieved
- prepare and make your contributions effectively
- encourage contributions from all participants
- take decisions.

This section covers:

Leading meetings	Page 142

Participating in meetings	Page 143

Meetings

Leading meetings

1. **Be clear about the purpose of the meeting** - do not call a meeting if there is a better way to solve a problem or make a decision.

2. **Invite the appropriate people to attend** - only invite those people who have something to contribute or gain, but make sure you invite all the people necessary to take decisions.

3. **Allow time for preparation** - carefully prepare how you will lead the meeting and talk to other members; circulate papers in advance so everyone can be well prepared.

4. **Clearly state the purpose of the meeting at the outset** - check that all attendees share the same purpose.

5. **Allocate sufficient time** - set a fixed time for the meeting to begin and end and allocate time appropriately for each item under discussion.

6. **Encourage all attendees to contribute** - use questioning skills and individual encouragement to ensure all views are represented.

7. **Discourage unhelpful comments and digressions** - be firm, but sensitive, in asking attendees to keep to the purpose of the meeting.

8. **Summarise** - summarise the discussion at appropriate times and allocate action points at the end of each item.

9. **Take decisions** - make sure that decisions are within the meeting's authority, that they are accurately recorded and promptly communicated to those who need to know.

10. **Evaluate the meeting** - allow time at the end of the meeting to evaluate whether the purpose of the meeting has been effectively achieved.

Meetings

Participating in meetings

1. **Prepare carefully** - get any papers or information in advance, and consult with others whom you are representing, so you can prepare how best to contribute to the meeting.

2. **Contribute effectively** - present your contributions clearly, accurately and at the appropriate time.

3. **Help to solve problems** - think about how you can help identify, clarify and come up with solutions to problems and help the meeting arrive at a valid decision.

4. **Keep to the point** - remember what the purpose of the meeting is and do not digress.

5. **Acknowledge the contributions and viewpoints of others** - acknowledge others' contributions and discuss these constructively, even if you disagree with them.

6. **Represent your group effectively** - if you are at the meeting as the representative of your organisation, department or team, make sure you fully represent their views, not just your own.

Managing Information

National Standards

What are National Standards?

National standards of performance, or 'occupational standards', have been developed for virtually all jobs in the UK today. The standards describe what people are expected to do in their jobs, and how they are expected to do them. There are, for example, occupational standards for retail staff, cooks, care workers, administrative staff, construction workers and those working in manufacturing and engineering industries.

The Management Standards, developed by the Management Charter Initiative (MCI), describe the standards of performance expected of managers and supervisors in their job roles. They also describe the knowledge base which managers need to be able to perform effectively. The Management Standards apply to all managers and supervisors, regardless of the sector in which they are working. Whilst the context may be different, the process of, say, counselling staff, budgeting or implementing a change programme will be similar in all industries.

The Management Standards are available at four different levels:

Standards	Qualification
Senior Management Standards	Under development
Middle Management Standards	NVQ/SVQ Level 5
First line Management Standards	NVQ/SVQ Level 4
Supervisory Management Standards	NVQ/SVQ Level 3

The Standards for Managing Energy describe the distinctive standards of performance expected of those with the specific responsibility to ensure the effective management of energy resources to meet the organisations objectives. They apply equally to those with the job title *Energy Manager* and to those with other job titles such as *Deputy Manager, Technical Manager, Operations Manager* etc who are clearly managing energy for a considerable part of their working day.

The Management Standards and the Standards for Managing Energy, like all occupational standards, have been developed for assessment purposes, particularly assessment leading to National Vocational

Qualifications (NVQs) or Scottish Vocational Qualifications (SVQs). Energy Managers who can prove they are competent in Units of the Standards for Managing Energy can gain credit for *additional units* to their NVQ or SVQ.

However, many organisations and their managers use the standards for a wide range of purposes, including recruitment and selection, training needs analysis, design of training programmes, performance review and appraisal, succession planning and promotion criteria. Organisations are now beginning to link them to quality initiatives such as ISO 9000, Total Quality Management and Investors in People.

The checklists for *Energy Management* are relevant to all those involved, either wholly or in part, with ensuring the effective management of energy resources. They are based largely on the Standards for Managing Energy (see pages 148-149) and other appropriate standards, such as those developed by the Purchasing and Supply Lead Body.

The checklists for *Operational Management* are relevant to all levels of management, although supervisors and first line managers may find they contribute to, rather than have full responsibility for, an activity. They are based mainly on the Middle Management Standards (see pages 150-151) and on other appropriate standards, such as those developed by the Customer Service Lead Body or the Training and Development Lead Body .

The links between the checklists and the different sets of standards are shown on pages 152-154.

Standards for Managing Energy

The Standards for Managing Energy define the standard of performance required of those with specific responsibility for ensuring the effective management of energy resources. They form the basis of the checklists for *Energy Management*.

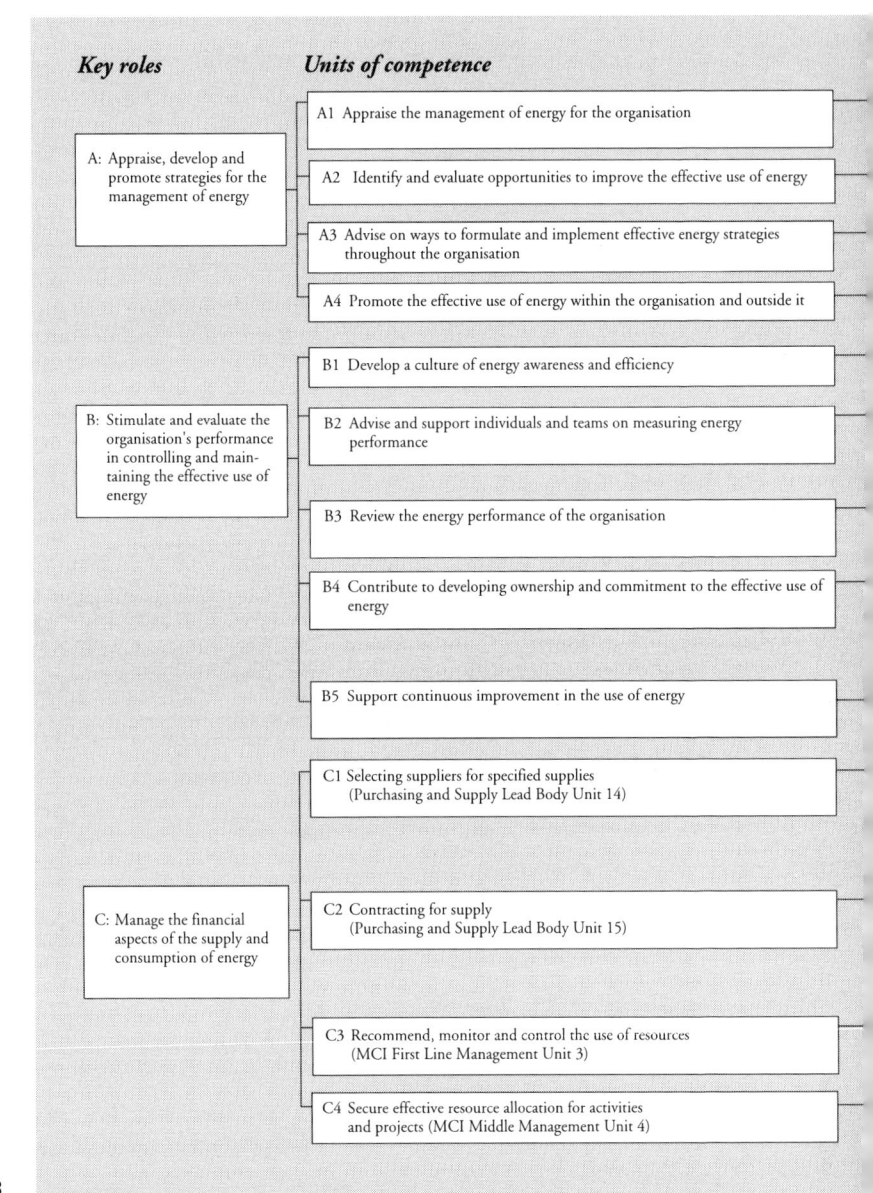

Key roles	Units of competence
A: Appraise, develop and promote strategies for the management of energy	A1 Appraise the management of energy for the organisation
	A2 Identify and evaluate opportunities to improve the effective use of energy
	A3 Advise on ways to formulate and implement effective energy strategies throughout the organisation
	A4 Promote the effective use of energy within the organisation and outside it
B: Stimulate and evaluate the organisation's performance in controlling and maintaining the effective use of energy	B1 Develop a culture of energy awareness and efficiency
	B2 Advise and support individuals and teams on measuring energy performance
	B3 Review the energy performance of the organisation
	B4 Contribute to developing ownership and commitment to the effective use of energy
	B5 Support continuous improvement in the use of energy
C: Manage the financial aspects of the supply and consumption of energy	C1 Selecting suppliers for specified supplies (Purchasing and Supply Lead Body Unit 14)
	C2 Contracting for supply (Purchasing and Supply Lead Body Unit 15)
	C3 Recommend, monitor and control the use of resources (MCI First Line Management Unit 3)
	C4 Secure effective resource allocation for activities and projects (MCI Middle Management Unit 4)

Elements of competence

- A1.1 Determine the organisation's current performance in the effective management of energy
- A1.2 Establish the organisation's performance and scope for improvement in the management of energy

- A2.1 Identify opportunities which improve energy efficiency
- A2.2 Evaluate and advise on opportunities which improve energy efficiency

- A3.1 Advise on the formulation of strategies which achieve an effective use of energy
- A3.2 Advise on ways to implement energy efficiency strategies throughout the organisation

- A4.1 Promote energy efficiency in the organisation
- A4.2 Promote the organisation's achievements in energy efficiency to others outside the organisation

- B1.1 Advise individuals and teams on energy efficient practices
- B1.2 Support a culture of energy awareness

- B2.1 Devise monitoring systems and processes to evaluate organisational performance in energy management
- B2.2 Enable individuals and teams to design and develop performance measurement systems
- B2.3 Support the collection, analysis, and documentation of information relating to energy usage

- B3.1 Collect, analyse and record information for energy efficiency performance
- B3.2 Determine the organisation's ongoing performance in energy efficiency

- B4.1 Support and encourage individuals and teams to improve their performance in effective energy usage
- B4.2 Advise on the competences needed to deliver the organisation's energy management plans
- B4.3 Advise on training requirements to maintain and improve competence in the effective use of energy

- B5.1 Evaluate information relating to continuous improvements in energy usage
- B5.2 Advise individuals and teams on developments and improvements in the effective use of energy

- C1.1 Select potential suppliers
- C1.2 Obtain bids
- C1.3 Obtain tenders
- C1.4 Clarify and improve offers
- C1.5 Decide on supplier after evaluation of offers

- C2.1 Negotiate supply agreement
- C2.2 Establish contract for supply agreement
- C2.3 Place contract for supply
- C2.4 Deal with contractual claims
- C2.5 Resolve variations in supply

- C3.1 Make recommendations for expenditure
- C3.2 Monitor and control the use of resources

- C4.1 Justify proposals for expenditure on projects
- C4.2 Negotiate and agree budgets

National Standards

Middle Management Standards

The Middle Management Standards define the standard of performance required of operational managers with a broad range of responsibility. They form the basis of the checklists for *Operational Management*.

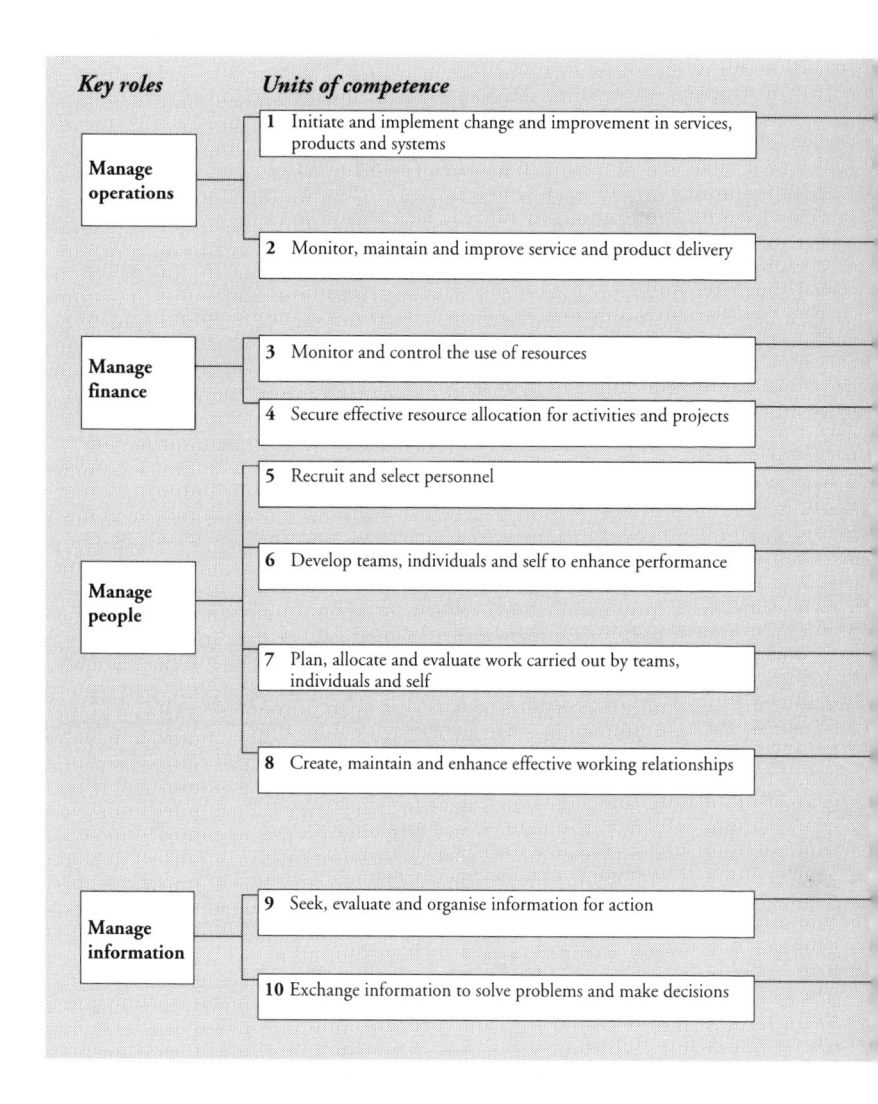

Key roles	*Units of competence*
Manage operations	1 Initiate and implement change and improvement in services, products and systems
	2 Monitor, maintain and improve service and product delivery
Manage finance	3 Monitor and control the use of resources
	4 Secure effective resource allocation for activities and projects
Manage people	5 Recruit and select personnel
	6 Develop teams, individuals and self to enhance performance
	7 Plan, allocate and evaluate work carried out by teams, individuals and self
	8 Create, maintain and enhance effective working relationships
Manage information	9 Seek, evaluate and organise information for action
	10 Exchange information to solve problems and make decisions

Elements of competence

1.1	Identify opportunities for improvement in services, products and systems
1.2	Evaluate proposed changes for benefits and disadvantages
1.3	Negotiate and agree the introduction of change
1.4	Implement and evaluate changes to services, products and systems
1.5	Introduce, develop and evaluate quality assurance systems

2.1	Establish and maintain the supply of resources into the organisation/department
2.2	Establish and agree customer requirements
2.3	Maintain and improve operations against quality and functional specifications
2.4	Create and maintain the necessary conditions for productive work activity

3.1	Control costs and enhance value
3.2	Monitor and control activities against budgets

4.1	Justify proposals for expenditure on projects
4.2	Negotiate and agree budgets

5.1	Define future personnel requirements
5.2	Determine specifications to secure quality people
5.3	Assess and select candidates against team and organisational requirements

6.1	Develop and improve teams through planning and activities
6.2	Identify, review and improve development activities for individuals
6.3	Develop oneself within the job role
6.4	Evaluate and improve the development processes used

7.1	Set and update work objectives for teams and individuals
7.2	Plan activities and determine work methods to achieve objectives
7.3	Allocate work and evaluate teams, individuals and self against objectives
7.4	Provide feedback to teams and individuals on their performance

8.1	Establish and maintain the trust and support of one's subordinates
8.2	Establish and maintain the trust and support of one's immediate manager
8.3	Establish and maintain relationships with colleagues
8.4	Identify and minimise interpersonal conflict
8.5	Implement disciplinary and grievance procedures
8.6	Counsel staff

9.1	Obtain and evaluate information to aid decision making
9.2	Forecast trends and developments which affect objectives
9.3	Record and store information

10.1	Lead meetings and group discussions to solve problems and make decisions
10.2	Contribute to discussions to solve problems and make decisions
10.3	Advise and inform others

National Standards

Links between the Checklists and the Standards

Energy Management Checklists	Standards for Managing Energy
Appraising Energy Management	
Assessing current energy management performance	A1.1
Assessing the scope for improvement	A1.2
Identifying and Evaluating Opportunities for Improvements	
Identifying opportunities to improve energy efficiency	A2.1
Evaluating and advising on opportunities to improve energy efficiency	A2.2
Providing Advice on Energy Strategies	
Providing advice on formulating strategies	A3.1
Providing advice on implementing strategies	A3.2
Measuring Energy Performance	
Developing monitoring systems and processes	B2.1
Collecting and recording information	B3.1
Assessing energy efficiency performance	B3.2
Promoting the Efficient Use of Energy	
Promoting energy efficiency in your organisation	A4.1
Publicising energy efficiency achievements	A4.2
Encouraging Commitment to Energy Efficiency	
Supporting and encouraging people to use energy more efficiently	B4.1
Providing advice on the skills required for the efficient use of energy	B4.2
Providing advice on training and development	B4.3
Providing Energy Efficiency Advice	
Providing advice on developing energy efficient plans	
Providing advice on energy efficient practices	B1.1
Providing Advice on Measuring Energy Performance	
Supporting the development of performance measurement systems	B2.2
Supporting the collection, analysis and documentation of information	B2.3
Supporting Continuous Improvement in Energy Usage	
Evaluating information relating to continuous improvement in energy usage	B5.1
Providing advice on developments and improvements in energy usage	B5.2
Selecting Suppliers	
Selecting potential suppliers	C1.1
Obtaining bids	C1.2
Obtaining tenders	C1.3
Clarifying and improving offers	C1.4
Deciding on supplier	C1.5
Contracting for Supply	
Negotiating supply agreement	C2.1
Establishing a contract for supply	C2.2
Placing a contract for supply	C2.3
Dealing with contractual claims	C2.4
Resolving problems in supply	C2.5

Links between the Checklists and the Standards

Operational Management Checklists	Middle Management	First Line Management	Supervisory Management
Meeting Customer Needs			
Establishing and agreeing customer requirements	2.2		
Maintaining supplies	2.1		
Maintaining a productive work environment	2.4	1.2	1.2
Meeting customer specifications	2.3	1.1	1.1
Solving problems for customers			
Managing Change			
Identifying opportunities for improvements	1.1		
Assessing the pros and cons of change	1.2	2.1	
Negotiating and agreeing the introduction of change	1.3		
Implementing and evaluating changes	1.4	2.2	
Quality Assurance			
Assuring quality	1.5		
Time Management			
Managing your time			
Personnel Planning			
Planning human resource requirements	5.1	4.1	3.1
Drawing up job specifications	5.2		
Assessing and selecting staff	5.3	4.2	3.1
Making staff redundant			
Developing Teams and Individuals			
Developing teams	6.1	5.1	4.1
Developing individuals	6.2	5.2	4.1
Developing yourself	6.3	5.3	4.4
Coaching			4.2
Mentoring			
Evaluating and improving training and development	6.4	5.2	4.3
Managing Teams and Individuals			
Planning work	7.2	6.2	5.1
Allocating work	7.3	6.3	5.2
Setting objectives	7.1	6.1	5.2
Giving feedback	7.4	6.4	5.3
Working Relationships			
Building a relationship with your manager	8.2	7.2	6.2
Building relationships with staff	8.1	7.1	6.1
Building relationships with colleagues	8.3	7.3	6.1
Minimising conflict	8.4	7.4	6.3
Managing Problems with Staff			
Counselling	8.6	7.6	
Implementing grievance and disciplinary procedures	8.5	7.5	6.4
Firing staff			
Equal Opportunities			
Promoting equal opportunities			
Encouraging diversity and fair working practices			

National Standards

Operational Management Checklists	Middle Management	First Line Management	Supervisory Management
Managing Budgets			
Preparing budgets	4.1	3.1	2.1
Negotiating and agreeing budgets	4.2		
Monitoring budgets	3.2	3.2	2.2
Cost Control			
Controlling costs	3.1	3.2	2.2
Using Information			
Obtaining and evaluating information	9.1	8.1	7.1
Recording and storing information	9.3	8.2	7.1
Forecasting trends and developments	9.2		
Presenting information and advice	10.3	9.3	7.2
Meetings			
Leading meetings	10.1	9.1	
Participating in meetings	10.2	9.2	

Keywords Index

Accidents
    accident procedure   76

Achievements
    publicising   33

Advice & guidance
    providing   11-28,37-38,41-43, 45-47,51,102,114, 139
    seeking   19,59,78,95,106, 112,119-120,123

Agreements
    budgets   129
    change   82
    customers   74
    suppliers   75

Aspirations
    of individuals   109

Assessment
    change   81
    facilitating   102
    people   14
    performance   28
    recruitment   94
    self-assessment   100,109
    tools & techniques   26

Assumptions
    budgets   129
    forecasts   138

Audience
    feedback   33,139
    presentations   33,139

Audits
    energy   15,51

Authority
    budgets   130,132
    limits of   107

Benefits (see Evaluating)

Bids
    for supply   57

Briefing
    on work   107

Budgets
    agreeing   129
    monitoring   130
    negotiating   129
    preparing   128

Championing
    energy efficiency   29-38

Change
    effects of   81,83
    implementation   83
    managing change   79-83
    monitoring   43
    pros and cons   81

Claims   65

Coaching   101

Conflict
    minimising   107,115
    with colleagues   114

Commitment
    to energy efficiency   14,32
    to equal opportunities   122
    to quality assurance   86

Communication
    with candidates   94
    with colleagues   82-83,86
    with customers   74,78,86
    with staff   32,86,95,119

Competitor
    activity   75
    for supply   58

Consultation
    with colleagues   78,92,93,139
    with manager   112
    with staff   86,92,95,98,106, 108,113,128
    with teams   98,106

Contingency
    planning   88,128
    allowances   129

Contract
    for supply   55-66

Corrective action
    expenditure   130,132
    income   130
    operations   42,77

Cost (see also Expenditure)
    control   131-132
    cost-effectiveness   83,98,99
    energy   23,32
    human resources   92

Counselling
    personal problems   118
    redundancy   95

Criteria
    selection   56,60,62,94

Culture
    of energy efficiency   22,32,33

Customers
    communication   74,78
    feedback   74,77
    needs, requirements   74,86
    problems   78

Debriefing
    after training   103

Decision-making
    change   81
    energy   23
    independent   102
    meetings   142
    time management   88

Delegating
    time management   88

Design   22

Development (see also Training & development)
    identification of needs   37,98-101

Digressions
    avoiding   143
    controlling   88
    discouraging   142

Direction
    degrees of   106

Discipline
    procedures   119-120

Discrimination
    challenging   123

Discussing problems and concerns
    with manager   112
    with staff   113,115

Dismissal   95,120

Disruptions
    minimising   77

Diversity
    of working styles   123

Encouragement
    contributions   142
    feedback   33,47,109
    mentoring   102
    performance   108

Energy management   7-66

Environment
    effect on   15,32
    sustainable   18

Equipment
    availability   76
    developments   80
    maintenance   76

Estimates
    income   128
    expenditure   128

Equal opportunities
    action plan   122
    diversity   93
    fair working practices   37,123
    policy   122
    procedures   94
    promoting equal
        opportunities   122
    recruitment   94
    redundancy   95

Evaluating
    benefits   22,32
    changes   83
    energy   18,23,51
    equal opportunities   122
    information   28,136
    meetings   142
    performance   43,109
    quality assurance   86
    training &
        development   38,103

Expenditure
    budgets   128-129
    estimates   128
    monitoring   130
    phasing   130
    variances   130

Experience
    learning from   74,80,81,83,103,107,
        115,119,128

Facilitating
    learning   102
    assessment   102

Feedback
    from customers   77
    from others   33,38,47,64,100,101
    to individuals   77,108,109,123
    to learners   101-102
    to teams   77,109

Finance
    managing   125-132

Firing staff   120

Forecasting
    energy performance   28
    trends and
        developments   78,80

Friction
    minimising   98

Grants	18
Grievance	
procedure	119
Human resource	
planning	91-95
Income	
budgets	128-129
estimates	128
monitoring	130
variances	130
Indicators	
performance	14
Information	
about customer problems	78
about developments	22,80
about grievance & disciplinary procedures	119
about threats & opportunities	112
evaluating	50,136
from suppliers	27
managing information	47,50,133-143
obtaining	27,136
on budgets	128,129
on costs	132
on customer needs	74
on energy usage	26,28,33,36,42,43, 46,47,50
on skills	37
planning	92
presenting information	82,139
recording	27,137
storing	137
Interruptions	
controlling	88
Involvement (see Consultation)	
Job specifications	93
Knowledge	
requirements	93
Law (legal requirements)	
agreements	55-66,74
Clean Air Act	14
COSHH	14
conflicts at work	115
Environmental Protection Act	14
equal opportunities	94,122-123
Fuel/Electricity Control Act	14
Health & Safety at Work Act	14
grievance & disciplinary procedures	119
job specifications	92
recruitment & selection	94
redundancy	95,120
work methods	106
workplace	76
Learning	
style	101
Maintenance	
equipment	76
requirements	22
Management Charter Initiative (MCI)	146-147,160
Materials	
developments	80
supplies	75,76
Measures	
of performance	26,46
Meetings	
leading	142
participating	143
Mentoring	102
Misconduct (gross)	120
Monitoring	
budgets	130
changes	83
energy performance	22,42,43,51
operations	77
processes & systems	15,26,43,50
National Vocational Qualifications (NVQs)	146-147
National Council for Vocational Qualifications (NCVQ)	160
Negotiation	
budgets	129
change	82
customers	74
suppliers	59,62,66,75
Networks	
developing	136
Objectives	
achievement	103,108
development	97-103
individual	88,93,108,112
learning	101-102
of negotiation	62
organisational	22,26,32,33, 106-107,115
Offers	
for supply	59-60

Operational management 67-143

Participation (see also
   **Commitment and
   Consultation**)
   change 82

People
   managing 89-123

Performance
   assessing 28,43,50
   encouraging 108,109
   measures 26,46,50
   measurement systems 46
   rating 60
   review 109
   standards 37

Personnel
   planning 91-95

Plans
   contingencies 88
   implementing change 82,83
   operational 77
   personnel 91-95
   presenting 82,83
   time 88
   work 106

Policy
   advice 112,139
   counselling 118
   customer problems 78
   organisational 56-66
   redundancy 95

Preparation
   for meetings 142-143

Presenting
   advice 139,143
   budgets 128
   information 139,143
   performance indicators 14
   plans 83,92

Price
   supplies 59,75

Priorities
   time management 88

Problems
   counselling 118
   customers 78
   discussing 111-115
   obstacles to change 80,83
   solving 78,142-143
   staff 117-120
   supplies 66

Procedures
   accident 76
   bids 57
   customer problems 78
   disciplinary 119-120,123
   effects on 15
   grievance 119
   improvements 80
   quality 86
   recruitment &
     selection 94
   redundancy 95
   tenders 58

Products
   provision of 74-75

Productivity 32,76

Promises
   to colleagues 114
   to staff 113

Promoting & publicising
   energy efficiency 32
   good practice 36

Proposals
   presenting 112

Purchasing
   energy 19,53-66

Quality
   assurance 85-86
   improvements 32,80
   service 75

Quotations
   from suppliers 56

Recognition
   of achievement 109
   of ideas, views,
     contributions 113,143

Recommendations
   improvements 19,28,36,79-83,132
   firing staff 120
   grievance & disciplinary
     procedures 119
   quality assurance 86
   recruitment &
     selection 94
   strategies 23
   working conditions 76

Records
   change 82
   conflicts 115
   contracts &
     agreements 56-66
   customers 74
   department 76
   expenditure 132
   feedback 109

grievance & disciplinary procedures	119	
information	137	
operation	77	
recruitment & selection	94	
suppliers	75	

Recruitment & selection 94

Recycling 18

Redundancy 95

Relationships
- with colleagues 114
- with manager 112
- with mentees 102
- with providers 38
- with staff 113

Representing
- others 143

Requirements
- statutory 14

Research (see also Review)
- customer needs 74

Resources
- developments 80
- effective use 77,83,86,98,99
- effects on 15
- identifying 23
- limitations 37,42
- review of 18
- supplies 76,77

Responsibility
- for energy efficiency 14,22,36
- individual 107,115
- job specifications 93
- team 107,115

Results (see Evaluating)

Review
- change 83
- customer problems 78
- development plans 98-99
- forecasts 138
- information requirements 136
- information storage 137
- job descriptions 93
- mentoring 102
- monitoring 19
- organisation performance 109
- progress 88
- suppliers 75

Safety 15

Satisfaction of customers 78,86

Savings
- energy 15

Schedules 77

Scottish Vocational Qualifications (SVQs) 146-147

SCOTVEC 160

Selection
- of staff 94

Services
- provision of 74-75

Skills
- coaching 101
- developing 97-103
- identification of needs 92

Special Needs
- costs 92
- identifying 122
- working environment 76

Specialists
- access 107
- advice 139
- equal opportunities 123
- grievance & disciplinary procedures 119
- job specifications 93
- training & development 98

Specifications
- for supply 57-59

Staff involvement (see Consultation)

Standards
- of behaviour 115
- of work 115
- Management Standards 146-154

Stereotyping
- discouraging 123

Strategies
- energy 14,22,23,28,33

Strengths
- individual 99,122
- self 100
- team 98

Summarising
- action points 142

Supervision
- of work 107

159

Suppliers		55-66,75
Support		
	energy efficiency	39-51
	for colleagues	36
	for learning	102
	for manager	112
	for mentees	102
	for staff	113
Targets		
	energy performance	22,46,50
Team		
	development	98,100
	management	105-109
	qualities required	92
Technology		
	change	18,19,80
Tender		
	for supply	58
Threats		
	information about	112
Time		
	efficient use	87-88
	for development	100
	for others	113-114
	management	87-88
	meetings	142
Training & development		
	costs	92
	energy efficiency	23,38
	equal opportunities	122
	evaluating	38,103
	individuals	99
	opportunities in work	107
	plans	98-100,103
	redundancy	95
	self	100
	teams	98
	use of equipment	76
Understanding		
	checking	83,86,107,108,113
Value		
	supplies	75
Values		
	of organisation	32,33
Waste		15
Weaknesses		
	individual	99
	self	100
	team	98

Work		
	allocation	107,115
	briefing	107
	environment	76
	methods	106
	supervision	107

Useful Addresses

Management Charter Initiative
Russell Square House
10-12 Russell Square
London WC1B 5BZ
Tel: 0171 872 9000
Fax: 0171 872 9099

National Council for Vocational Qualifications
222 Euston Road
London NW1 2BZ
Tel: 0171 387 9898
Fax: 0171 387 0978

SCOTVEC
Hanover House
24 Douglas Street
Glasgow G2 7NQ
Tel: 0141 248 7900
Fax: 0141 242 2244

The Institute of Energy
18 Devonshire Street,
London W1N 2AU
Tel: 0171 580 0077
Fax: 0171 580 4420